MEDIT

A Science-Backed Approach to Joyful, Healthy

Eating

JAMES MARINO

TABLE OF CONTENTS

Introduction

Imagine savoring a meal as vibrant and colorful as the Mediterranean coastline itself: a platter of ripe tomatoes drizzled with golden olive oil, a bowl of hearty lentils with fresh herbs, and a side of sun-ripened fruits. The Mediterranean diet is more than just a way of eating—it's a way of life that brings together tradition, culture, and health in perfect harmony. For thousands of years, people in Mediterranean regions have thrived on this diet, celebrating food as a source of both nourishment and joy. Now, science has caught up with this time-honored lifestyle, confirming that the Mediterranean diet doesn't just make meals delicious—it also makes lives healthier and more fulfilling.

In the modern world, where diet trends come and go, the Mediterranean diet stands apart. It isn't about strict rules, calorie counting, or deprivation; instead, it invites you to eat mindfully, enjoy a rich variety of foods, and make eating an act of celebration. This is a diet built on simple, wholesome ingredients: fresh vegetables and fruits, whole grains, legumes, fish, olive oil, and a sprinkling of nuts and seeds. But it's also built on something even more profound: a philosophy of balance and connection, both with nature and with others.

Over the past few decades, extensive research has uncovered the powerful health benefits of the Mediterranean diet. Studies have shown that it can reduce the risk of chronic diseases, support brain health, and even contribute to longer life expectancy. But beyond the science, there is a more personal, human side to this diet. It's about savoring each bite, relishing the aromas and flavors, and sharing food with friends and family around a table filled with laughter and love.

In this book, we will take a journey through the Mediterranean diet from all angles: its rich history, the science behind its benefits, and practical ways to bring this style of eating into your own life. You'll learn about the individual ingredients that make it so powerful, discover easy recipes that highlight its flavors, and find tips for adopting this lifestyle no matter where you live.

Above all, this book is about embracing joyful, healthy eating. Whether you're looking to improve your health, reconnect with your food, or simply explore a new culinary experience, the Mediterranean diet offers something unique—a pathway to a balanced, vibrant life.

So take a seat, relax, and get ready to discover how the Mediterranean way of eating can transform not only what you put on your plate but also how you live each day.

Chapter 1

The Foundation of the Mediterranean Diet

History and origins: Roots in Southern Europe, North Africa, and the Middle East

The origins of the Mediterranean diet stretch back thousands of years and encompass a vast, diverse region that includes Southern Europe, North Africa, and the Middle East. This region, which wraps around the Mediterranean Sea, has long been a crossroads of civilizations, each contributing its own agricultural practices, culinary traditions, and lifestyle habits. From ancient Greece and Rome to the Ottoman Empire,

Phoenicians, and Berbers, the interplay between these cultures fostered a unique culinary heritage that today forms the foundation of the Mediterranean diet.

The geography of the Mediterranean region has had a significant influence on the foods and farming practices that define its cuisine. With its warm, temperate climate, the area is ideal for growing olives, grapes, grains, and various fruits and vegetables, all staples of the Mediterranean diet. Olive trees, for instance, have been cultivated in the region for over 6,000 years, becoming both an economic and cultural symbol. Olive oil, derived from this ancient crop, is one of the defining elements of Mediterranean cuisine and is celebrated not only for its flavor but also for its health benefits. The region's coastal and mountainous landscapes allowed communities to cultivate a wide variety of crops while also supporting fishing and livestock rearing, leading to a diet rich in seafood, dairy, grains, and legumes.

In ancient Greece, diet and health were central concepts, and food was often seen as medicine. Greek physicians, including Hippocrates, advocated for diets that promoted balance and health, a principle that remains central to the Mediterranean diet today. Greeks emphasized the importance of fresh produce, whole grains, legumes, and moderate wine consumption—elements that remain prominent in modern Mediterranean cuisine. In addition, they celebrated olive oil, not only as a culinary ingredient but also for its medicinal properties. This connection between diet and well-being formed a foundation for the later development of Mediterranean eating practices and their emphasis on fresh, minimally processed foods.

Moving westward, the Romans expanded upon Greek agricultural techniques and food practices, spreading Mediterranean staples across their vast empire. Romans valued ingredients such as wheat, olives, and wine, creating a triad that became central to their diet and, eventually, to Mediterranean culture as a whole. Bread made from wheat became a staple food, particularly among the lower classes, while wine and olive oil were produced on a massive scale to meet the demands of the empire. Rome's expansion helped spread Mediterranean foods and practices throughout Southern Europe and parts of North Africa, embedding a common dietary pattern that would shape the cuisine of the region for centuries to come.

In North Africa, Berber communities contributed unique culinary practices and ingredients to the Mediterranean diet. Berbers cultivated grains such as wheat and barley, which they used to make staples like couscous and flatbreads, while also incorporating locally grown vegetables, legumes, and spices. North African cuisine introduced a wide array of spices—cumin, coriander, and saffron, among others—that added depth and complexity to Mediterranean dishes. The proximity to the desert led to creative preservation techniques, such as drying and fermenting, which ensured food was available even in harsh conditions. These methods, along with the use of aromatic spices and herbs, remain integral to the flavor profile of Mediterranean cuisine today.

The Middle East, with its ancient civilizations in Mesopotamia, Persia, and the Levant, contributed immensely to the Mediterranean diet's origins. Ancient Persians cultivated pomegranates, figs, and citrus fruits, all of which became symbolic of Mediterranean cuisine. Lentils, chickpeas, and other legumes were also staples in the Middle East, forming a rich protein source that complemented grains. The spread of

Islam in the 7th century facilitated trade routes that introduced rice, spices, and other goods from the Far East, further enriching Mediterranean cuisine. Middle Eastern cooking also emphasized communal eating, with meals often shared by large families and friends, a tradition that persists throughout the Mediterranean region and underscores the diet's emphasis on social connectedness.

The Ottoman Empire's expansion also played a significant role in shaping Mediterranean cuisine. The Ottomans brought together culinary influences from the Balkans, the Middle East, and North Africa, creating a rich tapestry of flavors and techniques. They introduced ingredients like eggplant and coffee to the Mediterranean, both of which became central to the region's cuisine. Ottoman cooking techniques, such as grilling and braising, along with the use of yogurt and a variety of spices, spread throughout the Mediterranean, integrating into local food traditions. The Ottomans also established trade networks that brought exotic spices and ingredients from Asia and Africa, further diversifying Mediterranean cuisine.

One of the hallmarks of the Mediterranean diet is its plant-based focus, a legacy rooted in the agricultural practices of the region. Because of the seasonal nature of Mediterranean agriculture, communities relied heavily on vegetables, grains, legumes, and fruits, with meat serving as a less frequent addition. In regions where fishing was accessible, seafood became a primary source of protein, particularly in coastal communities. This pattern of eating was shaped by necessity but eventually became a celebrated feature of the Mediterranean diet, one that aligns with modern health recommendations favoring plant-based foods and moderate protein consumption.

Culturally, the Mediterranean diet has always emphasized moderation, variety, and balance, principles that have been passed down through generations. For instance, fasting periods observed in Christianity and Islam influenced food traditions in the Mediterranean region. During these times, people abstained from animal products, focusing on plant-based foods and grains. These fasting practices not only reinforced a balanced approach to eating but also fostered creativity in developing flavorful, satisfying dishes using simple ingredients. This cultural backdrop contributes to the diet's emphasis on whole, minimally processed foods and its flexibility to incorporate various dietary needs and preferences.

In addition to food, the Mediterranean way of life emphasizes a slower, more mindful approach to eating. Meals are often enjoyed in a communal setting, with family and friends gathered around a table to share food, conversation, and laughter. This social aspect of eating fosters a sense of connection and well-being, reminding people to savor their meals and enjoy the experience of dining. It reflects the Mediterranean belief that food should be a source of pleasure and community rather than just sustenance. This practice remains central to Mediterranean life today and is a defining feature of the Mediterranean diet, underscoring the idea that food is best enjoyed in good company.

The blending of cultures around the Mediterranean Sea has also led to an appreciation for fresh, local ingredients, which form the backbone of Mediterranean cuisine. Unlike diets that rely on heavily processed foods, the Mediterranean diet emphasizes foods that are close to their natural state. From freshly caught fish to sun-ripened tomatoes, each meal celebrates the bounty of the region. Local markets, often bustling with vibrant displays of produce, seafood, and spices, remain a vital part of Mediterranean communities, providing a direct connection between people and the food they eat.

In the 20th century, the Mediterranean diet began to receive international attention when researchers noticed lower rates of heart disease among populations in countries like Greece and Italy compared to Western countries with more processed diets. Dr. Ancel Keys, an American scientist, conducted extensive research on this phenomenon, leading to the Seven Countries Study, which linked the Mediterranean diet to better cardiovascular health. This study popularized the diet and brought attention to its health benefits, inspiring people worldwide to adopt its principles.

Today, the Mediterranean diet is widely recognized for its health benefits, including reduced risk of heart disease, diabetes, and certain cancers, as well as improved mental health and longevity. It remains one of the most thoroughly studied and recommended dietary patterns, celebrated not only for its positive impact on physical health but also for its emphasis on social connection, cultural heritage, and enjoyment of life. The Mediterranean diet represents a powerful blend of ancient wisdom and modern science, offering a path to health that is as timeless as it is transformative.

In sum, the Mediterranean diet's roots in Southern Europe, North Africa, and the Middle East provide it with a rich tapestry of influences, each adding depth to its unique flavor profile and healthful properties. From the Greek and Roman empires to Berber and Middle Eastern traditions, the diet reflects a history of resilience, creativity, and respect for the land. Today, it continues to inspire people to live more healthfully and joyfully, honoring the age-old traditions that have shaped it. The Mediterranean diet is not only a testament to the cultural and culinary diversity of the region but also an enduring way of life that promotes balance, wellness, and a celebration of good food shared with others.

Cultural influences that shaped this dietary style

The Mediterranean diet is more than a simple eating plan; it is a tapestry woven from the diverse cultures that have existed around the Mediterranean Sea for thousands of years. This unique way of eating reflects the customs, agricultural practices, religious beliefs, and culinary techniques of various civilizations that have left their mark on the region. From the influence of ancient Greek philosophies to the food-sharing traditions of the Middle East, the Mediterranean diet is a product of rich cultural exchanges and evolving practices. Here, we explore some of the key cultural influences that have shaped this dietary style, creating a cuisine that is both diverse and deeply connected to the people who sustain it.

- **The Ancient Greeks: Food as Medicine and Philosophy**

Ancient Greek culture, with its emphasis on health, balance, and the "good life," contributed significantly to the foundation of the Mediterranean diet. Greeks like Hippocrates—the father of medicine—believed that food played a central role in health and well-being, viewing it as a form of preventive medicine. He and others advocated for simple diets that emphasized moderation, balance, and variety. Greek cuisine was based on fresh, local ingredients, including olive oil, bread, wine, and a range of fruits and vegetables, all of which remain staples in the modern Mediterranean diet.

The Greeks also promoted the concept of "symposia," or social gatherings centered around food and drink, where guests would share meals and engage in conversation. This tradition of communal eating, central to the Mediterranean diet today, reflects the Greek belief in food as a source of both sustenance and social connection. In addition, Greek myths and stories were often tied to food, with foods like grapes and olives gaining symbolic importance in cultural practices. These ancient beliefs about food's role in health, community, and pleasure have been passed down through generations, laying an early philosophical and cultural foundation for the Mediterranean diet.

- **Roman Influence: Bread, Olives, and Wine**

The Roman Empire further shaped the Mediterranean diet, solidifying the importance of bread, olives, and wine, which were considered staples of the Roman diet and economy. The Romans expanded agricultural practices across their empire, introducing olive cultivation to new regions and developing extensive trade networks that spread Mediterranean foodstuffs far and wide. Wheat, for example, became a cornerstone of the Roman diet, leading to the mass production of bread. Olive oil, used not only in cooking but also in religious and cultural ceremonies, became an essential part of daily life in the Roman world.

Roman culture also promoted the idea of "convivia," or feasts, where food and drink were shared communally. Feasts often included a variety of dishes made from local produce, seafood, and legumes, embodying the principles of variety and balance. The Roman approach to food, focused on both sustenance and pleasure, influenced the development of Mediterranean eating patterns long after the fall of the Roman Empire. Today, the legacy of Roman culinary practices can be seen in the continued importance of bread, olives, and wine as central elements of Mediterranean cuisine.

- **Berber Traditions in North Africa: Grains, Spices, and Preservation**

In North Africa, Berber communities contributed unique grains, spices, and preservation techniques that are now integral to Mediterranean cooking. Berbers, indigenous to the region, relied on grains such as barley, wheat, and sorghum, which they used to make staples like couscous and flatbreads. These grains provided a steady source of energy and were well-suited to the local climate. Additionally, the arid environment led to the development of food preservation methods, including drying, salting, and fermenting, which enabled people to store food and ensure a stable food supply throughout the year.

North African cuisine also introduced a variety of spices—such as cumin, saffron, and coriander—that are still widely used across the Mediterranean. These spices add complexity and depth to Mediterranean dishes, enriching the flavor profile while also offering health benefits, including antioxidant properties. Berber influence is still evident today in Mediterranean cuisine, with dishes like couscous and spice-rich tagines representing the rich flavors and resourceful practices of North African cultures.

- **The Middle East: Legumes, Shared Meals, and the Influence of Islam**

The Middle East, with its ancient civilizations and strategic location, contributed significantly to Mediterranean dietary traditions, particularly through the use of legumes, community-oriented meals, and religious practices. Legumes like lentils, chickpeas, and fava beans were staples in Middle Eastern diets, offering a rich source of protein and nutrients that complemented the region's grain-based dishes. Hummus, falafel, and other legume-based dishes became popular throughout the Mediterranean and remain dietary staples today.

The spread of Islam also influenced Mediterranean food practices, introducing fasting periods during Ramadan, when followers would refrain from eating during daylight hours. This led to the development of elaborate evening meals featuring dishes that are both nourishing and easy to share, a tradition that reinforced the communal aspect of dining in the region. Middle Eastern culinary practices also emphasized the use of spices, fresh herbs, and yogurt, all of which contribute to the distinctive flavors found in Mediterranean dishes today. Additionally, Islam's dietary laws shaped food choices and preparation techniques, fostering a mindful approach to eating that resonates in the Mediterranean lifestyle.

- **The Ottoman Empire: Fusion of Flavors and New Ingredients**

The expansion of the Ottoman Empire brought together cultures from the Balkans, the Middle East, and North Africa, creating a fusion of flavors, techniques, and ingredients that further diversified the Mediterranean diet. The Ottomans introduced ingredients like eggplant, coffee, and yogurt, which have since become central to Mediterranean cuisine. Ottoman culinary practices, including grilling, braising, and the use of yogurt-based sauces, became popular across the Mediterranean, influencing the preparation of meats, vegetables, and grains.

The Ottomans also played a key role in expanding trade routes, which allowed for the introduction of spices and ingredients from Asia and Africa. These trade networks helped incorporate new flavors into the Mediterranean diet, such as cinnamon, nutmeg, and pepper, enriching the already complex cuisine. The influence of Ottoman culture can still be seen in the widespread use of ingredients like yogurt and eggplant in Mediterranean dishes, as well as in cooking techniques that emphasize both simplicity and depth of flavor.

- **Spanish and Moorish Influence: Rice, Citrus, and the New World**

The Iberian Peninsula, influenced by both Spanish and Moorish cultures, added unique ingredients to Mediterranean cuisine, particularly rice and citrus. The Moors, who occupied Spain for centuries, introduced rice cultivation, which became a central part of Spanish cuisine and led to the creation of dishes like paella. The Moors also brought citrus fruits such as lemons and oranges, which were eventually grown throughout the Mediterranean region. These fruits, rich in vitamins and antioxidants, became essential to Mediterranean diets and are still celebrated for their health benefits.

In addition, Spanish explorers in the 15th and 16th centuries brought back ingredients from the New World, including tomatoes, peppers, and potatoes, which quickly found a place in Mediterranean cuisine. The integration of these ingredients created new flavor profiles and expanded the variety of Mediterranean dishes. Today, dishes like gazpacho, ratatouille, and many Italian pasta sauces owe their flavor and color to the tomatoes and peppers introduced by Spanish explorers.

- **Religious Traditions: Fasting, Feasting, and Dietary Laws**

Religious traditions have also significantly influenced Mediterranean dietary practices, particularly through fasting and feasting rituals. For instance, Christian Lent and Muslim Ramadan both involve periods of fasting, which encouraged the development of plant-based dishes that could be enjoyed when meat was restricted. These traditions fostered creativity with plant-based ingredients, leading to the rich array of vegetable, grain, and legume dishes that define Mediterranean cuisine.

In addition, dietary laws in Judaism and Islam shaped Mediterranean cooking practices by encouraging mindful choices about what could be consumed. These dietary restrictions promoted a diet rich in vegetables, grains, legumes, and fish, foods that remain staples in the Mediterranean diet today. Religious fasting and feasting not only influenced food choices but also strengthened the connection between food, community, and faith in Mediterranean cultures.

- **A Shared Philosophy of Balance and Enjoyment**

Across the Mediterranean region, a shared cultural philosophy emphasizes balance, moderation, and enjoyment in eating. Rather than focusing on restriction, Mediterranean cultures celebrate food as a gift to be enjoyed, a source of health, and a means of social connection. Mealtime traditions center on leisurely, communal dining, where people come together to savor flavors, enjoy each other's company, and create memories around the table.

This philosophy is perhaps the most significant cultural influence shaping the Mediterranean diet, promoting an approach to eating that values whole, fresh ingredients and a mindful relationship with food. Whether through small family gatherings or large community feasts, the Mediterranean way of eating reflects a commitment to both nourishment and pleasure, making it one of the world's most cherished and enduring dietary styles.

The Mediterranean diet, shaped by a wide range of cultural influences, is a testament to the resilience, adaptability, and diversity of the people who have lived around the Mediterranean Sea for centuries. From ancient Greeks to the Ottomans and beyond, each culture has left its mark on this unique way of eating, creating a diet that is both nutritionally balanced and richly flavorful. Today, the Mediterranean diet is celebrated for its health benefits and its joyful, inclusive approach to food—a lifestyle that continues to inspire people around the world.

Core foods: Vegetables, fruits, whole grains, legumes, nuts, olive oil, and seafood

The Mediterranean diet is widely celebrated for its health benefits and culinary diversity, largely due to its foundation in wholesome, nutrient-dense foods. These core foods—vegetables, fruits, whole grains, legumes, nuts, olive oil, and seafood—form the basis of a diet that is both sustainable and delicious. They not only provide a rich array of nutrients but also reflect the seasonal, local approach to eating that has defined Mediterranean life for centuries. Each of these foods brings unique flavors, textures, and health benefits, making the Mediterranean diet one of the most balanced and flavorful dietary patterns in the world. Below, we delve into each of these essential components, exploring their cultural significance, nutritional value, and role in Mediterranean cuisine.

- **Vegetables: The Heart of Mediterranean Meals**

Vegetables are at the heart of the Mediterranean diet, enjoyed at almost every meal and in various forms—raw, roasted, grilled, or stewed. Mediterranean cuisine celebrates the freshness and versatility of seasonal vegetables, which often include tomatoes, bell peppers, eggplant, zucchini, spinach, and leafy greens. These vegetables provide essential vitamins, minerals, fiber, and antioxidants, promoting heart health, improved digestion, and reduced inflammation.

The abundance of vegetable-based dishes reflects the traditional agricultural practices of the region, where farming communities relied on crops that could thrive in the Mediterranean climate. Dishes like Greek "horta" (wild greens), Italian caponata (a Sicilian eggplant stew), and ratatouille from France showcase the creativity with which

Mediterranean cultures use vegetables. Rather than serving as mere side dishes, vegetables often take center stage in Mediterranean meals, contributing both flavor and nutritional value to the diet.

- **Fruits: Nature's Sweetness and Antioxidant Power**

Fruits play an essential role in the Mediterranean diet, providing natural sweetness, essential vitamins, and powerful antioxidants. Seasonal fruits like oranges, grapes, figs, pomegranates, apples, and melons are enjoyed fresh or occasionally dried, contributing to the diet's balance of fiber and natural sugars. These fruits are often consumed as snacks or as simple desserts, a reflection of the Mediterranean emphasis on using whole, unprocessed foods.

In addition to their health benefits, fruits like grapes and pomegranates hold cultural significance in the Mediterranean region. Grapes are not only eaten fresh but also used to make wine, a traditional part of Mediterranean culture, especially in Southern Europe. Figs and pomegranates, long associated with ancient myths and cultural practices, symbolize fertility and abundance. The Mediterranean diet's reliance on fruits reinforces the value of eating locally and seasonally, as these fruits are enjoyed at their peak freshness, maximizing both their flavor and nutritional content.

- **Whole Grains: A Sustaining Source of Energy**

Whole grains, such as wheat, barley, oats, bulgur, and farro, are staple foods in the Mediterranean diet, providing a key source of energy and essential nutrients like fiber, B vitamins, and minerals. Unlike refined grains, whole grains retain their bran and germ, making them more nutritious and beneficial for heart health and digestion. Traditional Mediterranean foods like whole-grain bread, pasta, and rice-based dishes are central to the diet and are typically consumed in moderation.

Bread, often made from whole grains, has a special place in Mediterranean culture and is enjoyed with nearly every meal. In Greece, Italy, and other Mediterranean countries, whole-grain bread is used to scoop up olive oil, sauces, or dips, embodying the diet's focus on simplicity and flavor. Grains are also used in staple dishes like Italian farro salads, Spanish paella, and North African couscous, showcasing the region's ingenuity in creating satisfying meals from humble ingredients. The Mediterranean emphasis on whole grains supports a balanced intake of carbohydrates, ensuring a steady release of energy throughout the day.

- **Legumes: A Plant-Based Protein Powerhouse**

Legumes, including lentils, chickpeas, beans, and peas, are vital sources of protein, fiber, and iron in the Mediterranean diet. These plant-based proteins provide an affordable and sustainable alternative to meat, which is consumed sparingly in traditional Mediterranean meals. Legumes are celebrated for their versatility, appearing in a wide range of dishes across Mediterranean countries.

From chickpea-based hummus in the Middle East to Italian pasta e fagioli (pasta and beans) and Moroccan lentil stews, legumes serve as the foundation for many beloved Mediterranean dishes. Rich in complex carbohydrates, legumes help maintain balanced blood sugar levels and offer long-lasting energy, making them ideal for both health and sustenance. They are also an excellent source of soluble fiber, which supports heart health by helping to reduce cholesterol levels. The inclusion of legumes in the Mediterranean diet reflects a tradition of resourceful cooking that emphasizes nutrition, affordability, and flavor.

- **Nuts and Seeds: Nutrient-Dense Snacks and Toppings**

Nuts and seeds, including almonds, walnuts, pistachios, and sesame seeds, play an important role in the Mediterranean diet, providing healthy fats, protein, fiber, and various vitamins and minerals. These nutrient-dense foods are often enjoyed as snacks or used to enhance the flavor and texture of Mediterranean dishes. For example, almonds are commonly used in Spanish cooking, while sesame seeds appear in Middle Eastern tahini (sesame paste) and Greek desserts.

Walnuts, in particular, are prized in Mediterranean cuisine for their high omega-3 fatty acid content, which supports heart and brain health. Nuts and seeds also offer a satisfying crunch and a natural source of healthy fats, making them a valuable component of a balanced diet. Their versatility allows them to be incorporated into both sweet and savory dishes, whether sprinkled over salads, added to yogurt, or baked into traditional desserts. The Mediterranean diet's emphasis on nuts and seeds demonstrates a holistic approach to fats, favoring sources that are both nourishing and delicious.

- **Olive Oil: The Golden Elixir of the Mediterranean**

Olive oil is perhaps the most iconic food of the Mediterranean diet, renowned for its flavor and numerous health benefits. Rich in monounsaturated fats and antioxidants, olive oil is the primary fat source in Mediterranean cooking and is used generously in everything from dressings and marinades to sautéing vegetables and drizzling over finished dishes. The high antioxidant content of extra virgin olive oil contributes to reduced inflammation, improved heart health, and a lower risk of chronic diseases.

The production and use of olive oil are deeply rooted in Mediterranean history and culture. Olive trees, cultivated in the region for thousands of years, are seen as symbols of peace, wisdom, and resilience. In Mediterranean countries like Greece, Italy, and Spain, olive oil production is not only an agricultural practice but also a cultural heritage. The central role of olive oil in the Mediterranean diet reflects the region's preference for natural, minimally processed ingredients, and its focus on flavorful, health-promoting foods.

- **Seafood: A Lean Protein Rich in Omega-3s**

Seafood is another cornerstone of the Mediterranean diet, providing a lean source of protein and essential omega-3 fatty acids, which support heart and brain health. Due to the

Mediterranean Sea's proximity, fish and shellfish have been part of local diets for centuries. Unlike red meat, which is consumed in moderation, seafood is enjoyed regularly in Mediterranean cuisine, with popular choices including sardines, anchovies, salmon, and shellfish.

Mediterranean seafood dishes, such as Spanish paella, Greek grilled octopus, and Italian pasta with clams, highlight the natural flavors of fresh, local fish. Seafood is often prepared simply, seasoned with olive oil, lemon, and herbs to enhance its flavor without overpowering it. This emphasis on fresh, high-quality seafood aligns with the Mediterranean diet's focus on foods that are both nutritious and flavorful. The inclusion of fish and other seafood provides essential nutrients, such as iodine and selenium, which contribute to overall health and wellness.

- **A Harmonious Blend of Flavor and Nutrition**

Each of these core foods—vegetables, fruits, whole grains, legumes, nuts, olive oil, and seafood—brings its own unique benefits to the Mediterranean diet. Together, they create a diet that is rich in vitamins, minerals, healthy fats, and fiber, offering a harmonious balance of macronutrients and antioxidants that support longevity and vitality. The Mediterranean diet's emphasis on variety and seasonal produce ensures that meals are both nutritionally balanced and deliciously diverse, making healthy eating an enjoyable, sustainable lifestyle.

These core foods also reflect the Mediterranean's deep connection to the land, the sea, and the people who cultivate and prepare them. By relying on fresh, local ingredients, the Mediterranean diet fosters a sense of community and environmental stewardship. Whether through the shared experience of a family meal or the simple pleasure of a ripe tomato, the Mediterranean diet offers a way of life that honors both health and heritage, creating a nourishing foundation for generations to come.

Chapter 2

The Science Behind the
Mediterranean Diet

Deep dive into scientific research on the diet's impact on heart health, cognitive function, and longevity

Over recent decades, the Mediterranean diet has captured global attention for its health benefits, consistently emerging as one of the healthiest dietary patterns in scientific studies. Extensive research has revealed that the diet's nutrient-rich, plant-forward approach has profound effects on heart health, cognitive function, and longevity. Each of these areas has been the subject of rigorous scientific investigation, leading to evidence-based conclusions that highlight the Mediterranean diet's positive influence on overall health and quality of life. Here, we explore the findings of scientific studies on the Mediterranean diet, delving into its impact on cardiovascular wellness, cognitive preservation, and extended lifespan.

- **Heart Health: Reducing the Risk of Cardiovascular Disease**

Cardiovascular health is one of the most extensively studied aspects of the Mediterranean diet, with numerous research findings affirming its cardioprotective properties. The diet's emphasis on plant-based foods, healthy fats, and lean proteins supports heart health by reducing cholesterol, lowering blood pressure, and decreasing inflammation. The high intake of monounsaturated fats from olive oil, coupled with omega-3 fatty acids from fish, plays a crucial role in lowering levels of

LDL (bad) cholesterol while increasing HDL (good) cholesterol, which collectively reduces the risk of atherosclerosis.

One of the most notable studies in this area is the PREDIMED (Prevención con Dieta Mediterránea) trial, a landmark study conducted in Spain that examined the effects of a Mediterranean diet on cardiovascular risk among over 7,000 participants at high risk for heart disease. The study found that those who followed a Mediterranean diet enriched with extra-virgin olive oil or nuts had a 30% lower risk of experiencing a heart attack, stroke, or death from cardiovascular causes compared to those who followed a low-fat diet. This trial underscored the importance of specific components of the Mediterranean diet—such as olive oil and nuts—as essential contributors to heart health.

Additionally, the Mediterranean diet's rich array of fruits, vegetables, whole grains, and legumes provides antioxidants and fiber, which work together to reduce inflammation and improve blood vessel function. These anti-inflammatory effects help mitigate the risk of hypertension and other cardiovascular conditions. The Mediterranean diet's protective benefits against cardiovascular disease have been validated in numerous observational studies and clinical trials, cementing its role as a heart-healthy diet.

- **Cognitive Function: Enhancing Memory and Protecting Against Neurodegenerative Diseases**

Another area of growing research on the Mediterranean diet is its potential to enhance cognitive function and delay the onset of neurodegenerative diseases such as Alzheimer's and Parkinson's. Studies have demonstrated that the diet's nutrient-dense profile, abundant in antioxidants, healthy fats, and anti-inflammatory compounds, supports brain health by protecting neurons, enhancing communication between brain cells, and reducing oxidative stress, which is linked to cognitive decline.

One prominent study on this topic, published in the journal Neurology, followed 1,000 older adults and found that those who adhered closely to a Mediterranean diet had slower rates of cognitive decline compared to those who did not. Participants who consumed higher amounts of leafy greens, berries, olive oil, and fish—a combination of foods typical of the Mediterranean diet—performed better on cognitive tests, showing stronger memory and attention spans. The diet's emphasis on polyphenol-rich foods such as fruits, vegetables, nuts, and wine provides powerful antioxidants that help reduce oxidative stress, a key factor in the aging process of brain cells.

The Mediterranean diet's impact on cognitive health is further supported by studies linking it to lower levels of beta-amyloid plaques and tau tangles in the brain, which are markers of Alzheimer's disease. The anti-inflammatory properties of omega-3 fatty acids, found in fatty fish and walnuts, and the brain-boosting effects of flavonoids in berries and leafy greens are believed to protect against these neurodegenerative markers. Collectively, these findings suggest that the Mediterranean diet's components work synergistically to preserve cognitive function, making it one of the most recommended diets for brain health.

- **Longevity: A Lifestyle that Supports a Longer, Healthier Life**

The Mediterranean diet's impact on longevity has been widely studied, with evidence showing that individuals who follow this dietary pattern tend to live longer, healthier lives. The diet's high intake of whole foods, combined with a reduced emphasis on processed items and red meat, promotes cellular health and reduces the risk of chronic diseases, contributing to extended lifespan and a better quality of life.

Research conducted on populations in Mediterranean regions, such as the island of Ikaria in Greece and Sardinia in Italy—both known as "Blue Zones" for their high concentrations of centenarians—has highlighted the Mediterranean diet's role in promoting longevity. Studies in these regions reveal that people who adhere to traditional Mediterranean diets have lower rates of chronic diseases like heart disease, diabetes, and cancer, which are major contributors to premature death. The diet's plant-heavy focus, rich in antioxidants, fiber, and phytonutrients, provides cellular protection and supports metabolic health, which are crucial for aging gracefully.

In a study published in the British Medical Journal, researchers followed over 20,000 middle-aged individuals and found that adherence to the Mediterranean diet was associated with a 25% reduction in all-cause mortality over a 10-year period. This study, among others, underscores that the Mediterranean diet's effects go beyond individual health markers to influence overall longevity. Key factors include the diet's ability to maintain balanced blood sugar levels, reduce inflammation, and minimize oxidative stress—processes that are fundamental to healthy aging.

Furthermore, the Mediterranean diet promotes a lifestyle of moderation, physical activity, and social connection, which together support not only physical but also mental health. These lifestyle factors, alongside nutrient-dense foods, contribute to what researchers describe as "compression of morbidity"—a reduction in the period of illness and frailty in old age, allowing people to enjoy a higher quality of life for longer.

- **Key Nutritional Components Supporting Health and Longevity**

  Monounsaturated Fats: Predominantly found in olive oil, monounsaturated fats lower LDL cholesterol levels, reducing the risk of cardiovascular diseases and contributing to brain health.

  Polyphenols and Antioxidants: Present in fruits, vegetables, and nuts, these compounds reduce oxidative stress and inflammation, supporting heart health, cognitive function, and cellular longevity.

Fiber: Found in whole grains, fruits, and legumes, fiber helps regulate blood sugar levels, promotes digestion, and supports cardiovascular health by lowering cholesterol.

Omega-3 Fatty Acids: Abundant in fatty fish and walnuts, omega-3s are essential for reducing inflammation, protecting brain cells, and preventing cognitive decline.

Polyunsaturated and Plant-Based Proteins: Sources like legumes, nuts, and seeds contribute essential nutrients that support muscle and metabolic health, reducing the risk of age-related diseases.

- **A Diet for Life: Scientific Validation of the Mediterranean Lifestyle**

The scientific research on the Mediterranean diet provides compelling evidence of its role in promoting heart health, preserving cognitive function, and supporting longevity. Unlike restrictive diets, the Mediterranean diet's flexibility, rich flavors, and emphasis on whole foods make it both enjoyable and sustainable, qualities that contribute to its widespread appeal. Studies from around the world have shown that adopting this dietary pattern, even later in life, can have substantial benefits, reducing the risk of chronic diseases and enhancing quality of life.

As research continues to uncover new insights, the Mediterranean diet remains at the forefront of recommended dietary patterns for its comprehensive health benefits. Its focus on balance, variety, and community reflects a lifestyle that nurtures both body and mind, offering a path to a healthier, longer life. The Mediterranean diet's enduring popularity, validated by scientific findings, positions it as a powerful tool for individuals seeking not only to improve their health but also to embrace a vibrant, fulfilling way of life.

Explanation of how Mediterranean foods support gut health, reduce inflammation, and balance blood sugar

The Mediterranean diet is a powerhouse of nutrients known for their holistic benefits, supporting everything from heart health to longevity. Among its many positive effects, the diet's impact on gut health, inflammation reduction, and blood sugar balance is especially significant. The core foods of the Mediterranean diet—rich in fiber, healthy fats, antioxidants, and low-glycemic carbohydrates—are particularly beneficial for these areas of health. Here, we explore the scientific explanations behind how Mediterranean foods promote gut health, reduce chronic inflammation, and help maintain stable blood sugar levels, contributing to overall wellness.

- **Gut Health: Nurturing a Healthy Microbiome**

A healthy gut is essential for digestion, immunity, and even mental health, and the Mediterranean diet's focus on fiber-rich, plant-based foods supports the growth of beneficial gut bacteria. Fiber serves as food for these bacteria, which produce short-chain fatty acids (SCFAs) when they ferment dietary fiber in the colon. SCFAs, such as butyrate, have been shown to strengthen the gut lining, reduce inflammation, and support a balanced microbiome. Vegetables, fruits, whole grains, legumes, and nuts, which are all staples in the Mediterranean diet, provide a diverse array of fibers that foster microbial diversity in the gut, an important factor in overall gut health.

Studies indicate that individuals following a Mediterranean diet have a higher diversity of gut bacteria compared to those who follow a Western diet, which is often low in fiber and high in processed foods. This diversity is linked to improved digestion, lower levels of inflammation, and even better mental health outcomes. For example, polyphenols found in olives, berries, and nuts act as prebiotics, promoting the growth of beneficial gut bacteria while inhibiting the growth of harmful pathogens. In this way, the Mediterranean diet helps maintain a balanced gut microbiome, which is key to supporting immune function, absorbing nutrients effectively, and reducing the risk of gastrointestinal diseases.

- **Reducing Inflammation: Fighting Chronic Diseases at the Source**

Chronic inflammation is a risk factor for many conditions, including heart disease, diabetes, arthritis, and neurodegenerative diseases. The Mediterranean diet's high intake of anti-inflammatory foods, such as olive oil, fatty fish, nuts, and antioxidant-rich vegetables, works to combat inflammation at the cellular level. Extra-virgin olive oil, a primary source of fat in the Mediterranean diet, contains high levels of oleocanthal, a compound with natural anti-inflammatory properties similar to ibuprofen. Oleocanthal, along with other antioxidants found in olives, helps inhibit inflammatory pathways in the body, reducing the risk of chronic disease.

Omega-3 fatty acids from seafood, especially fatty fish like salmon, sardines, and mackerel, are also essential for reducing inflammation. These fats reduce the production of inflammatory molecules and promote the release of compounds that resolve inflammation. This helps protect the body from low-grade, chronic inflammation, which can lead to oxidative stress and contribute to conditions like heart disease and diabetes. In addition to these sources, the Mediterranean diet's rich supply of vegetables, fruits, nuts, and seeds provides a steady intake of polyphenols and vitamins like vitamin C and E, which protect cells from oxidative damage and support the body's natural anti-inflammatory responses.

In a study published in The American Journal of Clinical Nutrition, participants who adhered to a Mediterranean diet showed lower levels of C-reactive protein (CRP), an inflammatory marker associated with cardiovascular disease, compared to those who followed a Western diet. This reduction in CRP highlights the Mediterranean diet's effectiveness in managing inflammation, providing a dietary approach to combating chronic inflammation and enhancing overall health.

- **Balancing Blood Sugar: Stable Energy and Lower Risk of Diabetes**

The Mediterranean diet is particularly effective in supporting balanced blood sugar levels, making it beneficial for people with type 2 diabetes or those at risk. Its low-glycemic approach, relying on whole grains, legumes, vegetables, and healthy fats, prevents rapid spikes in blood sugar, leading to more stable energy levels and reduced insulin resistance over time. Unlike refined carbohydrates, which are quickly broken down and absorbed, the complex carbohydrates in the Mediterranean diet are digested slowly, leading to a gradual release of glucose into the bloodstream.

Whole grains like barley, farro, and quinoa, as well as fiber-rich vegetables and legumes, slow the absorption of glucose and improve insulin sensitivity. Fiber, a key nutrient in these foods, not only promotes fullness but also reduces post-meal blood sugar spikes. Nuts and seeds, which are low in carbohydrates but high in protein, healthy fats, and fiber, also play a role in managing blood sugar by providing steady, long-lasting energy without elevating glucose levels dramatically. These foods, often eaten as snacks or added to meals, help maintain stable blood sugar and reduce cravings for high-sugar foods.

Olive oil, a central fat source in the Mediterranean diet, further supports blood sugar control by reducing insulin resistance, a condition in which the body's cells become less responsive to insulin, causing blood sugar levels to rise. In fact, a study published in Diabetes Care found that people who followed a Mediterranean diet were 52% less likely to develop type 2 diabetes than those who followed a low-fat diet. The combination of fiber-rich carbohydrates, healthy fats, and low levels of refined sugar makes the Mediterranean diet a highly effective approach for balancing blood sugar and reducing the risk of metabolic diseases.

- **Key Nutrients and Foods Supporting Gut Health, Inflammation Reduction, and Blood Sugar Balance**

  Fiber-Rich Foods: Vegetables, fruits, whole grains, and legumes provide soluble and insoluble fiber, which feed beneficial gut bacteria, reduce inflammation, and slow glucose absorption.

  Polyphenols: Found in olives, berries, nuts, and leafy greens, polyphenols support gut health by acting as prebiotics and combat inflammation through their antioxidant properties.

  Omega-3 Fatty Acids: Present in fatty fish like salmon and sardines, omega-3s reduce inflammatory markers and protect against chronic inflammation and metabolic disorders.

Monounsaturated Fats: Olive oil is rich in monounsaturated fats, which reduce LDL cholesterol, improve insulin sensitivity, and reduce inflammation.

Low-Glycemic Carbohydrates: Whole grains, legumes, and non-starchy vegetables help stabilize blood sugar, reducing the risk of insulin resistance and type 2 diabetes.

- **Holistic Health Benefits of Mediterranean Foods**

The Mediterranean diet's ability to promote gut health, reduce inflammation, and maintain balanced blood sugar levels makes it an excellent choice for both disease prevention and daily wellness. By focusing on a variety of nutrient-dense, anti-inflammatory foods, the Mediterranean diet offers a balanced approach to health that supports the body at a cellular level, reducing the risk of chronic conditions associated with inflammation, gut imbalances, and blood sugar spikes.

The Mediterranean diet's emphasis on fresh, unprocessed foods—along with lifestyle factors like physical activity and communal meals—fosters a holistic, sustainable approach to health. With its abundance of fiber, healthy fats, and low-glycemic carbohydrates, the Mediterranean diet supports not only physical well-being but also mental and emotional wellness, creating a comprehensive blueprint for lifelong health.

Overview of studies showing the mental health benefits of a Mediterranean-style diet

The Mediterranean diet is well-regarded for its positive effects on physical health, but growing research has also highlighted its significant impact on mental health. Studies across various populations indicate that adhering to a Mediterranean-style diet is associated with lower rates of depression, anxiety, and cognitive decline, as well as improved mood and mental well-being. The diet's balanced, nutrient-rich profile—which emphasizes whole foods, healthy fats, antioxidants, and fiber—nourishes the brain and supports mental health in a way that few other dietary patterns can match. Here, we explore the research demonstrating the mental health benefits of the Mediterranean diet and examine how this eating style contributes to emotional resilience and cognitive wellness.

- **Reducing Depression: How Mediterranean Foods Support Emotional Health**

One of the most widely studied areas of the Mediterranean diet's impact on mental health is its potential to reduce symptoms of depression. Depression is a complex mental health condition influenced by genetic, environmental, and lifestyle factors, including diet. The Mediterranean diet's abundance of anti-inflammatory foods—such as fruits, vegetables, whole grains, nuts, seeds, and olive oil—helps reduce chronic inflammation, a factor increasingly linked to depression. Foods rich in omega-3 fatty acids, like fatty fish and walnuts, are particularly beneficial, as omega-3s have been shown to enhance mood-regulating brain chemicals, such as serotonin and dopamine.

A groundbreaking study published in BMC Medicine (known as the SMILES trial) investigated the effects of a Mediterranean-style diet on adults with major depression. The participants who followed a Mediterranean diet for 12 weeks showed significant improvement in their depressive symptoms compared to those who continued with their usual diet. Roughly 32% of the diet group achieved remission from depression, compared to only 8% in the control group. This study, among others, suggests that the Mediterranean diet's nutrient profile may directly contribute to alleviating depressive symptoms by reducing inflammation and supporting healthy neurotransmitter function.

Furthermore, the Mediterranean diet's low glycemic load helps stabilize blood sugar levels, reducing mood swings and fatigue. By avoiding spikes and crashes in blood sugar, the diet supports a more stable mood and reduces irritability, both of which are essential for mental well-being.

- **Combating Anxiety and Stress: The Role of Nutrient-Dense Foods**

Anxiety disorders, like depression, are influenced by numerous factors, including diet. The Mediterranean diet's high intake of magnesium-rich foods—such as leafy greens, nuts, seeds, and whole grains—helps reduce anxiety by calming the nervous system and supporting a balanced stress response. Magnesium is essential for brain health, and studies have shown that deficiencies in this mineral are associated with higher rates of anxiety and even panic attacks. Additionally, B vitamins, which are plentiful in whole grains, legumes, and lean proteins, support the production of neurotransmitters that regulate mood, such as serotonin.

A study published in Psychiatry Research found that young adults who adopted a Mediterranean-style diet experienced reductions in anxiety symptoms and reported improved mood compared to those who continued with their typical Western diets. The Mediterranean diet's emphasis on whole foods and reduced intake of processed foods, which are often high in sugar and artificial additives, plays a role in supporting mental clarity and reducing stress. High-sugar diets can exacerbate anxiety symptoms by causing blood sugar fluctuations and increasing oxidative stress, whereas the Mediterranean diet's balanced, nutrient-dense foods help keep stress levels in check.

Another notable factor is the Mediterranean diet's inclusion of foods rich in antioxidants, such as berries, leafy greens, and olive oil. Antioxidants protect brain cells from oxidative stress, which can contribute to anxiety. The presence of these neuroprotective compounds has been shown to support emotional resilience, allowing individuals to better manage stress and anxiety in daily life.

- **Enhancing Cognitive Health: Protecting Against Cognitive Decline and Dementia**

Cognitive decline and neurodegenerative diseases, such as Alzheimer's and Parkinson's, are increasingly common in aging populations. Research suggests that the Mediterranean diet may offer a protective effect against cognitive decline, preserving memory, and supporting mental sharpness. The diet's high levels of antioxidants, polyphenols, omega-3 fatty acids, and vitamins contribute to brain health by reducing oxidative stress and inflammation, both of which are factors in cognitive decline.

A large study published in Neurology found that participants who adhered more closely to a Mediterranean diet had better cognitive performance and a slower rate of cognitive decline compared to those who followed Western diets. The researchers noted that individuals who consumed high levels of olive oil, fish, fruits, and vegetables showed greater resistance to age-related cognitive deterioration. The anti-inflammatory effects of these foods, along with their protective impact on neurons, appear to slow the progression of Alzheimer's and other forms of dementia.

Another study, part of the PREDIMED trial, found that older adults who supplemented their Mediterranean diets with extra-virgin olive oil or mixed nuts demonstrated better cognitive function and memory performance than those who followed a lower-fat diet. The Mediterranean diet's ability to enhance cognitive function is largely attributed to the combined effects of its core foods, which together promote brain health through multiple pathways. Omega-3 fatty acids from fish, for example, support brain cell structure, while polyphenols in olives, berries, and wine protect against neuroinflammation, helping preserve cognitive abilities.

- **Improving Overall Mood and Quality of Life**

Beyond its effects on specific mental health conditions, the Mediterranean diet also enhances overall mood and quality of life. Its nutrient-dense, whole-food approach promotes a steady energy supply, reducing fatigue and irritability while enhancing general well-being. The diet's anti-inflammatory, antioxidant-rich foods support emotional balance and may even reduce the risk of mood disorders.

Research published in Molecular Psychiatry highlighted that people following a Mediterranean-style diet had a 33% lower risk of developing depressive symptoms over a 10-year period. The study suggested that the Mediterranean diet's combination of vitamins, minerals, healthy fats, and complex carbohydrates helps to prevent mental health issues by ensuring that the brain receives the essential nutrients it needs. The sense of community and enjoyment often associated with the Mediterranean diet—through shared meals and culinary traditions—also contributes to mental wellness, fostering connections that are protective against feelings of loneliness and depression.

A social aspect that is sometimes overlooked but integral to the Mediterranean diet is the role of mealtime as a communal experience. Eating meals with family and friends is common in Mediterranean cultures and has been shown to promote social support and reduce feelings of isolation, both of which are vital for mental health. These social and cultural factors contribute to the diet's holistic approach to mental wellness, creating a lifestyle that not only sustains the body but also nurtures the mind.

- **Key Nutrients and Foods Supporting Mental Health**

Omega-3 Fatty Acids: Found in fatty fish, walnuts, and flaxseeds, omega-3s reduce inflammation and support neurotransmitter function, improving mood and cognitive health.

Antioxidants and Polyphenols: Present in fruits, vegetables, olive oil, and nuts, these compounds protect brain cells from oxidative stress, supporting mental resilience and cognitive function.

B Vitamins and Magnesium: Abundant in leafy greens, whole grains, and legumes, these nutrients support stress regulation and reduce anxiety.

Fiber-Rich Foods: Legumes, whole grains, and vegetables provide fiber that supports gut health, which in turn positively affects mood and mental clarity through the gut-brain axis.

Low-Glycemic Carbohydrates: Whole grains and vegetables promote stable blood sugar, helping to prevent mood swings and maintain a steady energy supply.

- **A Comprehensive Approach to Mental Wellness**

The Mediterranean diet's nutrient-rich, anti-inflammatory, and balanced approach to eating provides a foundation for mental well-being that goes beyond basic nutrition. Through its emphasis on whole foods, healthy fats, and antioxidants, the diet supports brain health, reduces symptoms of depression and anxiety, and protects against cognitive decline. Research indicates that this dietary pattern can play a pivotal role in promoting emotional stability and cognitive resilience, making it a powerful tool for mental health support.

The Mediterranean diet's benefits for mental health extend beyond individual nutrients to a lifestyle of balance, social connection, and mindful eating. Together, these factors create a holistic approach to wellness that nurtures both body and mind, supporting a healthier, more fulfilling life. As research continues, the Mediterranean diet remains an evidence-backed pathway for those seeking not only physical health but also enhanced mental and emotional well-being.

Chapter 3

A Day in the Life: What Mediterranean Eating Looks Like

Meal structure: Breakfast, lunch, and dinner examples, plus mindful snacking

The Mediterranean diet, celebrated for its focus on fresh ingredients, balanced nutrition, and heart-healthy fats, is more than a list of foods; it's a way of structuring meals that enhances both taste and well-being. Following a Mediterranean eating pattern includes prioritizing plant-based foods, whole grains, healthy fats, lean proteins, and occasional indulgences in moderation. Let's explore a typical Mediterranean meal structure for breakfast, lunch, and dinner, with options for mindful snacking to keep energy steady throughout the day.

- **Breakfast: Energizing and Nutrient-Rich**

In the Mediterranean diet, breakfast is often light yet nourishing, focusing on whole grains, fresh fruits, and dairy. The goal is to start the day with foods that provide sustained energy, fiber, and protein. One classic breakfast choice is Greek yogurt topped with fresh berries and a sprinkle of nuts or seeds. Greek yogurt, rich in probiotics and protein, aids in digestion and keeps you feeling full longer. The berries, packed with antioxidants and fiber, add natural sweetness, while the nuts provide healthy fats and protein. A drizzle of honey can add sweetness without overloading on refined sugars.

Another popular Mediterranean breakfast option is whole-grain toast with avocado and cherry tomatoes. Avocado, a great source of healthy monounsaturated fats, combines with the fiber-rich whole grain toast to create a filling meal. Cherry tomatoes add color, antioxidants, and a refreshing taste. For those who prefer something warm, a frittata made with eggs, spinach, and feta cheese can be a perfect choice. Eggs provide high-quality protein, spinach offers iron and fiber, and feta cheese adds a tangy flavor along with calcium. Adding herbs like parsley or basil can elevate the taste while contributing additional vitamins.

- **Lunch: Balanced and Flavorful**

Lunch in the Mediterranean diet is typically the main meal, often enjoyed with family or friends and featuring a variety of flavors and textures. A common Mediterranean lunch includes a hearty salad, often called a "village salad," which combines fresh tomatoes, cucumbers, olives, and feta cheese, drizzled with extra-virgin olive oil. This salad is not just filling but also provides essential vitamins, healthy fats, and fiber. Adding grilled chicken or chickpeas can boost the protein content, making it a balanced and satisfying meal.

Another lunch option is a Mediterranean grain bowl, which features ingredients like quinoa or farro, paired with roasted vegetables such as zucchini, bell peppers, and eggplant. The grains are rich in fiber and minerals, while the vegetables add antioxidants and vitamins. Topping the bowl with a tahini or lemon-garlic dressing enhances the flavors and provides healthy fats from the olive oil or sesame. For those seeking a more traditional dish, a portion of vegetable-stuffed peppers is a popular Mediterranean choice. These peppers can be filled with a mixture of rice, herbs, tomatoes, and pine nuts, offering a nutritious and visually appealing meal. A side of hummus with whole-grain pita bread can complete this lunch by adding a creamy, protein-packed dip made from chickpeas, tahini, and lemon.

- **Dinner: Light and Satisfying**

Dinner in the Mediterranean diet is usually lighter than lunch, focusing on easily digestible foods that aid in a restful night's sleep. A grilled fish with a side of steamed vegetables is a popular Mediterranean dinner choice. Fish such as salmon, trout, or sardines are rich in omega-3 fatty acids, which support heart and brain health. Pairing the fish with a side of steamed vegetables like asparagus, broccoli, or carrots provides fiber, vitamins, and minerals without weighing down the digestive system.

For a vegetarian option, a vegetable and legume stew made with lentils, tomatoes, onions, and bell peppers is a filling yet light dinner choice. Lentils provide protein and fiber, while the vegetables supply a range of vitamins and minerals. A sprinkle of parsley or basil enhances both the flavor and the nutrient profile. Another beloved dinner option in Mediterranean cuisine is a simple pasta dish, made with whole-grain pasta, cherry tomatoes, garlic, and a sprinkle of Parmesan cheese. This dish can be prepared with olive oil, which is a staple in Mediterranean cooking and contributes to satiety without excess calories. Adding a handful of arugula or spinach to the pasta gives a boost of greens and fiber, creating a balanced yet light meal.

- **Mindful Snacking: Keeping Energy Steady**

Mindful snacking is an integral part of the Mediterranean diet. Unlike traditional snacking, which can involve processed foods and sugary treats, Mediterranean snacks focus on nutrient-rich options that provide energy and keep hunger at bay. Fresh fruit is a popular choice for a midday snack, with apples, oranges, and grapes being easy, portable options that supply natural sugars, fiber, and antioxidants. Pairing fruit with a handful of nuts, such as almonds or walnuts, adds healthy fats and protein, creating a more balanced snack.

Another excellent Mediterranean snack is a small portion of hummus with sliced vegetables like cucumbers, carrots, and bell peppers. This combination provides fiber, protein, and healthy fats without being too calorie-dense. Hummus, made from chickpeas, tahini, and olive oil, is rich in protein and fiber, while the vegetables are refreshing and low in calories. For those with a sweet tooth, a piece of dark chocolate (70% cocoa or higher) paired with a few walnuts or almonds can be a satisfying and heart-healthy snack. Dark chocolate contains antioxidants that benefit heart health, and pairing it with nuts provides a dose of healthy fats that can help satisfy cravings.

- **Practical Tips for Adopting the Mediterranean Meal Structure**

Following the Mediterranean meal structure goes beyond individual food choices. It emphasizes mindful eating, enjoyment of meals, and a balanced approach to food. To integrate this style of eating, consider meal prepping to ensure that fresh fruits, vegetables, whole grains, and lean proteins are readily available. This can make it easier to avoid processed snacks and meals, keeping the diet aligned with Mediterranean principles.

Another key aspect is portion control, especially with higher-calorie foods like nuts, cheese, and olive oil. These foods are staples in the Mediterranean diet, but they are best enjoyed in moderation to prevent excessive calorie intake. Drinking water throughout the day and limiting sugary drinks are also central to the Mediterranean way of eating. Finally, eating with family or friends, when possible, can enhance the experience, turning meals into a time for social connection and relaxation.

The Mediterranean diet's meal structure offers a well-rounded approach to daily eating, focusing on nutrient-dense foods that benefit both the body and mind. Whether starting the day with Greek yogurt and berries, enjoying a hearty salad at lunch, or finishing with a light fish dinner, each meal reflects the Mediterranean emphasis on freshness, flavor, and balance. Mindful snacking with fruits, nuts, and hummus completes the picture, keeping energy levels stable and satisfying hunger between meals. Embracing this meal structure can lead to improved well-being and a more enjoyable relationship with food.

Comparison to typical Western eating habits

The Mediterranean diet has long been praised for its health benefits, emphasizing whole foods, heart-healthy fats, and a balanced approach to meals. In contrast, typical Western eating habits often focus on convenience, processed foods, and higher intake of refined sugars and unhealthy fats. This comparison explores the key differences between these two dietary patterns, particularly in food choices, meal structure, and overall health implications. While both diets include elements that can support health, the Mediterranean approach's emphasis on natural, nutrient-dense foods sets it apart as a lifestyle as much as a diet.

- **Food Choices: Whole Foods vs. Processed Options**

One of the most striking differences between the Mediterranean and Western diets is the selection of ingredients. The Mediterranean diet centers around whole foods—fresh fruits and vegetables, whole grains, legumes, nuts, seeds, lean proteins like fish and poultry, and high-quality fats from sources such as olive oil. These ingredients provide a broad range of essential nutrients, including vitamins, minerals, antioxidants, and healthy fats, all of which contribute to overall well-being and longevity. Processed foods are rare, if not avoided altogether, and sugar intake is generally low, often limited to occasional treats or natural sources like honey and fruit.

In contrast, Western diets tend to rely more heavily on processed and convenience foods, including refined grains, sugary snacks, and high-fat meats. Packaged foods, frozen meals, and sugary beverages are staples for many in the Western world, largely because of their accessibility, affordability, and ease of preparation. However, these options are often high in sodium, saturated fats, and added sugars while being low in fiber, vitamins, and other essential nutrients. Consuming processed foods regularly can lead to nutrient deficiencies and increased health risks, such as heart disease, diabetes, and obesity. While the Mediterranean diet encourages an abundance of plant-based foods and minimal processing, the Western diet's reliance on processed items has become one of its most defining characteristics.

- **Fat Sources: Healthy Fats vs. Saturated and Trans Fats**

Another major distinction between the Mediterranean and Western diets lies in their sources of dietary fat. In the Mediterranean diet, healthy fats, primarily monounsaturated fats from olive oil and polyunsaturated fats from fish, nuts, and seeds, form a large portion of the daily intake. Olive oil is a cornerstone, not only for cooking but also for dressings and drizzling over dishes, providing essential fatty acids that support heart health and reduce inflammation. Fatty fish like salmon and sardines are also common, rich in omega-3 fatty acids that contribute to cardiovascular health and cognitive function.

Western diets, however, tend to contain higher amounts of saturated fats and trans fats. These are often found in fried foods, fast food, baked goods, and processed meats like bacon, sausages, and cold cuts. Unlike the Mediterranean diet, which uses fats to enhance flavor and improve nutritional quality, the Western diet's saturated and trans fats are linked to a higher risk of heart disease, obesity, and inflammation. Additionally, Western cooking practices often rely on oils that can be detrimental to health, such as hydrogenated oils and margarine, which are high in trans fats and have been shown to raise cholesterol levels. This difference in fat sources is a significant factor in the varying health outcomes between these dietary patterns.

- **Protein Sources: Plant-Based and Lean Options vs. Red Meat**

The Mediterranean diet's protein sources are often plant-based, with regular use of legumes, nuts, and seeds, alongside lean meats like chicken and fish. Red meat is consumed infrequently, usually limited to special occasions or small portions. This pattern not only reduces saturated fat intake but also supports heart health and reduces the risk of chronic diseases. Fish, especially oily fish like mackerel and salmon, plays a central role, providing protein and essential omega-3 fatty acids.

Western diets, on the other hand, are typically higher in red and processed meats, which are often consumed multiple times a week, if not daily. Fast-food burgers, steaks, and processed meats like sausages are common sources of protein. These foods, while protein-rich, also come with high levels of saturated fat, cholesterol, and sodium, all of which can increase the risk of heart disease, cancer, and other health issues. By focusing on lean and plant-based proteins, the Mediterranean diet offers a more balanced approach that supports long-term health and reduces exposure to harmful compounds often associated with red and processed meats.

- **Carbohydrates: Whole Grains vs. Refined Carbs**

Carbohydrates form a crucial part of both dietary patterns but are approached quite differently. The Mediterranean diet emphasizes complex carbohydrates from whole grains, such as brown rice, quinoa, farro, and whole-grain pasta. These grains are high in fiber, vitamins, and minerals, and they release energy more slowly than refined grains, leading to sustained energy levels and better blood sugar control. Whole grains are typically served in moderation, complementing a meal rich in vegetables and healthy fats.

Conversely, the Western diet often relies on refined carbohydrates, such as white bread, pasta, and sugary cereals. These foods are low in fiber and nutrients and can lead to rapid blood sugar spikes, followed by crashes, contributing to overeating and weight gain. Processed foods in the Western diet frequently contain hidden sugars and refined grains, contributing to an increased risk of diabetes and metabolic syndrome. By prioritizing whole grains over refined ones, the Mediterranean diet supports stable energy and provides a more nutritious foundation for daily meals.

- **Meal Structure: Social and Mindful Eating vs. On-the-Go Convenience**

The Mediterranean approach to meals is often communal and mindful, emphasizing the enjoyment of food and social connection. Meals are typically shared with family or friends, and the eating experience is unrushed, encouraging mindfulness and connection. This structure allows people to be more attuned to their hunger and fullness cues, which can help prevent overeating and promote satisfaction. Mediterranean meals are often balanced, with a focus on variety and colorful plates that appeal to the senses, making each meal an enjoyable experience.

In contrast, Western eating habits are often characterized by convenience and speed. Fast food and quick, on-the-go meals are common, especially for lunch and dinner, as many people eat at their desks or in their cars. This pattern of eating can lead to a disconnection from the food itself, causing individuals to eat quickly and sometimes in excessive quantities. Additionally, the Western diet's focus on convenience often results in fewer meals shared with others, reducing the social and emotional benefits that can come from eating together. The Mediterranean focus on mindful, communal eating helps reinforce healthy eating behaviors that support both physical and mental well-being.

- **Health Implications: Longevity and Disease Prevention vs. Increased Chronic Disease Risk**

The health outcomes associated with these two diets reflect their contrasting structures and food choices. Numerous studies have shown that the Mediterranean diet is linked to lower risks of heart disease, obesity, type 2 diabetes, and certain types of cancer. Its emphasis on antioxidants, fiber, healthy fats, and nutrient-rich foods supports a long, healthy life and is associated with lower mortality rates. The Mediterranean diet is also known for its anti-inflammatory properties, thanks to high intake of omega-3 fats, polyphenols, and fiber, which together help reduce the risk of chronic inflammation—a key factor in many modern diseases.

Western eating habits, with their reliance on processed foods, unhealthy fats, and added sugars, have been linked to higher rates of obesity, heart disease, diabetes, and metabolic syndrome. The high intake of red meat, refined grains, and sugary drinks has contributed to the rise in chronic diseases, placing a significant burden on healthcare systems and affecting quality of life for many individuals. The Western diet's pro-inflammatory components, such as trans fats, sugar, and processed foods, contribute to a cycle of poor health outcomes and increased risk of early mortality.

The Mediterranean diet and typical Western eating habits differ significantly in their approach to food choice, meal structure, and overall health effects. While the Mediterranean diet promotes longevity and disease prevention through whole, nutrient-dense foods and a mindful approach to eating, the Western diet's focus on convenience, processed foods, and higher saturated fats has contributed to increased rates of chronic disease. For those looking to improve their health, adopting elements of the Mediterranean diet can offer a sustainable, enjoyable, and health-promoting alternative to the traditional Western dietary pattern.

How to enjoy meals socially, a key aspect of the Mediterranean way of eating

Sharing meals with family and friends is central to Mediterranean culture, creating a sense of community and enhancing the dining experience. This practice not only enhances meal enjoyment but also provides numerous mental, emotional, and physical health benefits. In a world where eating is often rushed or done alone, adopting the Mediterranean habit of social eating can help people cultivate healthier relationships with food and with each other.

- **The Tradition of Family Meals**

One key component of Mediterranean social eating is the tradition of family meals. Meals are seen as opportunities for family members to come together, often involving multiple generations. These shared meals allow for a sense of connection, continuity, and shared values that are deeply rooted in Mediterranean culture. Family meals are typically leisurely and enjoyed around a table, where conversation is just as important as the food itself. This setting fosters strong family bonds, creates a positive dining atmosphere, and promotes mindful eating, allowing everyone to fully appreciate their food. Whether it's a Sunday family lunch or a casual weekday dinner, this commitment to eating together offers a meaningful break from daily responsibilities.

Western cultures can benefit greatly from embracing this Mediterranean habit of prioritizing family meals. By designating specific times for meals, families can ensure that everyone has the opportunity to connect and unwind, even during busy weekdays. When families sit down together, they're also more likely to choose healthier foods, as shared meals naturally encourage a focus on balanced and satisfying options.

- **Celebrating Meals with Friends and Neighbors**

In addition to family gatherings, the Mediterranean diet emphasizes the joy of sharing food with friends and neighbors. Whether it's a weekend picnic or a holiday celebration, Mediterranean meals often bring people together in relaxed, convivial settings. Mediterranean people are known for their hospitality, often inviting friends and neighbors to join them in meals and celebrations. These gatherings allow for laughter, storytelling, and the building of community bonds, creating lasting memories tied to the enjoyment of food. Each dish is shared with others, rcinforcing the idea that food is a means of connecting with others, not just a source of sustenance.

Bringing this Mediterranean approach into daily life can be as simple as organizing occasional dinners with friends, hosting a potluck, or enjoying a meal outdoors with neighbors. By creating opportunities for social dining, people can foster friendships, relieve stress, and appreciate the pleasures of good food in good company. This practice can transform meals from solitary events into vibrant, shared experiences, nurturing both body and soul.

- **Dining Without Distractions**

Social eating in Mediterranean culture also involves dining without distractions. In a traditional Mediterranean setting, meals are often free from interruptions like television, smartphones, or other digital devices. This creates an environment where everyone at the table can engage in meaningful conversations and fully enjoy the flavors and textures of their food. By focusing on each other and the meal, diners are able to practice mindful eating, which helps them better appreciate what they are eating and recognize when they are full. This approach promotes healthier eating patterns, as individuals are less likely to overeat or eat out of boredom.

For those looking to incorporate Mediterranean practices, establishing tech-free mealtimes can help create a more focused and enjoyable dining experience. By setting aside devices and distractions, families and friends can fully engage in each other's company and savor the moment, creating a shared experience that adds to the satisfaction of the meal.

- **Seasonal and Local Ingredients: Celebrating the Bounty Together**

In the Mediterranean, meals often celebrate seasonal and local ingredients, which brings a sense of appreciation and connection to nature's rhythms. Dining together over a meal made from fresh, seasonal ingredients reinforces the joy of eating foods at their peak ripeness and flavor. This practice not only enhances the taste of the meal but also contributes to a sustainable approach to eating. Meals are often simple yet flavorful, relying on fresh herbs, ripe tomatoes, vibrant greens, and other ingredients that are abundant in the season, creating a communal celebration of the harvest.

Incorporating this practice into everyday life can bring a sense of appreciation and excitement to the table. Exploring local farmers' markets or growing a small garden allows people to bring fresh ingredients to their meals, celebrating each season's unique flavors. Preparing and enjoying these meals with family or friends can create lasting memories and add a deeper level of satisfaction to the dining experience.

- **Rituals Around Meals: Enhancing the Dining Experience**

In the Mediterranean region, meals are often surrounded by small rituals that enhance the experience. Whether it's starting with a shared blessing, clinking glasses in a toast, or beginning with a small appetizer, these rituals help to create a sense of ceremony around eating. These practices give meals a sense of significance and encourage everyone to slow down, savoring each course. Rituals like toasting or saying grace can also help set a positive tone for the meal, allowing everyone to pause and appreciate the company and food.

Adding similar rituals into daily life can elevate the dining experience. Simple acts like lighting a candle, setting the table with care, or beginning the meal with a toast can make each meal feel more special. These small touches help people move away from rushed meals and instead create moments of gratitude, relaxation, and connection with others.

- **Creating a Balanced Plate: A Shared Mediterranean Practice**

In the Mediterranean diet, meals are typically balanced, with an array of colorful vegetables, grains, proteins, and healthy fats presented on the table. Sharing a variety of dishes allows everyone to try different flavors and encourages balanced eating. This focus on variety and abundance promotes a sense of satisfaction without overeating, as people can enjoy smaller portions of each food and avoid monotony. The balance and diversity of Mediterranean meals make them naturally appealing and nourishing, supporting both body and mind.

Adopting this balanced approach to meals can make shared dining experiences more enjoyable and fulfilling. By including a range of flavors, colors, and textures, meals become a sensory delight, adding to the pleasure of eating together. This approach also encourages healthier choices, as diners are more likely to enjoy nutrient-dense foods when they are presented as part of a colorful and varied meal.

- **The Benefits of Social Eating for Mental Health**

  Social eating in the Mediterranean culture is closely associated with mental and emotional well-being. Shared meals provide a sense of belonging, reduce stress, and foster positive feelings, as people experience the warmth and companionship of others. Studies have shown that eating in a social setting can improve mood, decrease feelings of loneliness, and even enhance cognitive health. The act of preparing, sharing, and enjoying food together strengthens social bonds, which is essential for mental health and resilience.

  Incorporating social eating into daily life offers a chance to experience these benefits. Regular shared meals with family or friends, whether daily or weekly, can foster a sense of community, joy, and connection, helping to alleviate the isolation often felt in modern, fast-paced lifestyles. By creating space for social interactions around meals, individuals can enjoy the comfort and support that come from eating together.

- **Embracing the Mediterranean Approach to Social Eating in Modern Life**

While it may seem challenging to implement Mediterranean social eating practices in today's busy world, small steps can make a big difference. Embracing even one shared meal a day, preparing foods with loved ones, or designating tech-free dinners are simple yet impactful ways to incorporate the Mediterranean way of eating. Whether it's gathering friends for a weekend brunch, hosting a dinner party, or cooking with family, these practices bring people together and make meals a joyful and health-promoting experience.

The Mediterranean approach to social eating teaches us that meals can be much more than a way to satisfy hunger—they can be an opportunity to connect, celebrate, and enjoy the simple pleasures of good food and good company. By taking time to share meals with others, people can foster meaningful relationships, improve mental well-being, and adopt healthier, more mindful eating habits. Embracing these practices can bring a piece of Mediterranean warmth and joy into everyday life, enhancing both the dining experience and overall quality of life.

Chapter 4

The Essentials of Mediterranean Cooking

Essential pantry staples: olive oil, herbs, legumes, grains, and more

Having a well-stocked pantry with key Mediterranean staples makes it easier to prepare balanced, flavorful meals that align with this diet's principles. Ingredients like olive oil, fresh herbs, legumes, and grains are central to the Mediterranean way of eating, each bringing unique health benefits and culinary versatility. These staples provide the foundation for Mediterranean cooking, allowing you to create a wide variety of satisfying dishes that reflect the richness of the region's cuisine.

- **Olive Oil: The Heart of Mediterranean Cooking**

Extra virgin olive oil is often considered the cornerstone of the Mediterranean diet. It's used generously in cooking, drizzled over dishes, and even enjoyed with bread. Olive oil is rich in healthy monounsaturated fats, which are known to support heart health by lowering bad cholesterol (LDL) and raising good cholesterol (HDL). Additionally, it contains polyphenols, which have antioxidant and anti-inflammatory properties that may help protect against chronic diseases.

To make the most of olive oil's benefits, it's best to use high-quality extra virgin olive oil. This versatile oil can be used in countless ways: as a base for salad dressings, a finishing touch for roasted vegetables, or a way to add depth to cooked grains.

Keeping olive oil as a pantry staple makes it easy to incorporate healthy fats into daily meals, giving dishes a distinctive Mediterranean flavor and health boost.

- **Herbs and Spices: Flavorful and Nutrient-Rich Additions**

Herbs and spices play a significant role in Mediterranean cuisine, adding vibrant flavors without extra calories or salt. Fresh herbs like basil, oregano, rosemary, and thyme are commonly used, as well as spices such as cumin, coriander, and paprika. These ingredients not only enhance the taste of dishes but also offer numerous health benefits. For example, oregano and rosemary are packed with antioxidants, while cumin and turmeric have anti-inflammatory properties.

Herbs and spices can be used in a variety of ways, from seasoning roasted vegetables to marinating proteins and flavoring soups. Keeping a variety of fresh and dried herbs on hand adds flexibility to cooking and allows for a diverse range of flavors in everyday meals. Adding these simple, nutrient-rich ingredients can turn basic ingredients into flavorful dishes with minimal effort.

- **Legumes: A Plant-Based Protein Powerhouse**

Legumes, including lentils, chickpeas, beans, and peas, are an essential source of protein and fiber in the Mediterranean diet. They are inexpensive, versatile, and packed with nutrients like iron, folate, and magnesium. Legumes are often used as a base for salads, soups, and stews, or they can be blended into spreads like hummus. Due to their high fiber content, legumes help keep you feeling full and satisfied, supporting both digestive health and weight management.

Dried or canned legumes are ideal pantry staples, as they have a long shelf life and can be incorporated into a wide range of recipes. For example, chickpeas can be added to salads, stews, or roasted as a snack, while lentils are perfect for hearty soups. By incorporating legumes into meals regularly, you can add a plant-based protein source that is both nutritious and satisfying.

- **Whole Grains: Sustained Energy and Essential Nutrients**

Whole grains are another key component of the Mediterranean diet, providing sustained energy, fiber, and essential nutrients. Common grains include bulgur, farro, barley, quinoa, and brown rice, all of which are high in fiber and have a lower glycemic index than refined grains. These grains are nutrient-dense, offering B vitamins, iron, magnesium, and antioxidants that support heart health, digestion, and overall well-being.

Whole grains can serve as the base for salads, side dishes, and even main courses. They pair well with vegetables, herbs, and proteins, making them a versatile choice for balanced meals. Keeping a variety of whole grains in the pantry ensures that you always have a healthy and satisfying option on hand, whether you're making a grain salad, a bowl, or a side dish.

- **Nuts and Seeds: Healthy Fats and Crunchy Texture**

Nuts and seeds, such as almonds, walnuts, sunflower seeds, and chia seeds, are commonly used in the Mediterranean diet. They provide a concentrated source of healthy fats, protein, fiber, and essential nutrients like vitamin E, magnesium, and zinc. Walnuts, in particular, are rich in omega-3 fatty acids, which support heart and brain health. Nuts and seeds add crunch and depth to dishes and can be used in various ways, from topping salads to blending into sauces.

Because they are calorie-dense, nuts and seeds are typically enjoyed in moderate amounts, often as a topping or snack rather than a main ingredient. Keeping a selection of nuts and seeds in the pantry allows for easy, nutrient-packed additions to meals. For example, sprinkling almonds on a salad or adding chia seeds to yogurt can boost both flavor and nutritional value.

- **Tomatoes and Tomato-Based Products: A Mediterranean Staple**

Tomatoes are a staple in Mediterranean cuisine, known for their vibrant color and tangy flavor. Whether fresh, canned, or made into sauces, tomatoes add depth to many dishes and are rich in vitamins C, K, and potassium, along with the powerful antioxidant lycopene, which has been linked to heart health and reduced cancer risk. Tomato-based sauces, such as marinara, are widely used in pasta dishes, stews, and as bases for many Mediterranean recipes.

Having canned tomatoes, tomato paste, or jarred marinara sauce on hand ensures you have a quick base for flavorful dishes. Fresh tomatoes are also a staple for salads and can be roasted or grilled to enhance their natural sweetness. Incorporating tomato-based products into your pantry offers endless options for creating delicious and nutritious meals.

- **Garlic and Onions: Aromatic and Health-Boosting Ingredients**

Garlic and onions are essential in Mediterranean cooking, providing a base for countless recipes. These aromatic ingredients not only add depth and complexity to dishes but also have numerous health benefits. Garlic, in particular, contains allicin, a compound known for its immune-boosting and anti-inflammatory effects. Onions are high in antioxidants and have been linked to improved heart health and reduced inflammation.

Garlic and onions can be used in nearly every meal, from sautéing them as a base for soups and sauces to roasting them alongside vegetables. These ingredients are inexpensive and versatile, making them essential pantry staples for anyone following the Mediterranean diet. Their flavors enhance the natural taste of other ingredients, allowing for rich, satisfying dishes without the need for excessive seasoning.

- **Vinegar and Citrus: Bright Flavors and Digestive Benefits**

Vinegar, particularly balsamic, red wine, and apple cider varieties, is frequently used in Mediterranean cooking to add acidity and depth to dishes. Combined with olive oil, vinegar forms the base of simple, flavorful dressings for salads and marinades. Citrus fruits like lemons and oranges are also essential, bringing a bright, tangy flavor to meals. Rich in vitamin C and antioxidants, citrus fruits contribute to immune health and add a refreshing element to both savory and sweet dishes.

Keeping a few types of vinegar and fresh lemons in the pantry ensures that you can quickly create dressings, marinades, or finishing touches for dishes. The acidity of vinegar and citrus enhances the flavors of other ingredients, while their health benefits make them valuable additions to a balanced diet.

- **Building a Mediterranean Pantry for Flavorful, Balanced Meals**

Having a pantry stocked with Mediterranean staples allows you to prepare wholesome, flavorful meals that align with the diet's principles. These ingredients provide the foundation for balanced, satisfying dishes and support a variety of cooking techniques and flavors. With essentials like olive oil, fresh herbs, legumes, and whole grains, you have the flexibility to create meals that reflect the vibrant, health-promoting aspects of Mediterranean cuisine.

By focusing on these simple, nutrient-rich ingredients, you can create a kitchen environment that supports healthy eating and culinary enjoyment. The versatility and health benefits of these staples make it easy to adopt the Mediterranean diet in daily life, offering a delicious and nourishing way to cook, eat, and live.

Simple techniques for cooking Mediterranean-style at home

You don't need complicated equipment or extensive culinary experience to cook Mediterranean-style at home. By focusing on fresh ingredients and using straightforward techniques, you can bring the vibrant flavors and health-promoting qualities of the Mediterranean to your meals. Simple methods like roasting, grilling, sautéing, and marinating allow the natural flavors of vegetables, proteins, and grains to shine while keeping meal preparation easy and enjoyable.

- **Embracing Olive Oil as a Base for Flavor**

Extra virgin olive oil is a staple in Mediterranean cooking and serves as a flavorful base for many dishes. Rich in healthy fats, olive oil enhances the taste of foods while adding depth and richness. Rather than relying on butter or heavy sauces, olive oil is used for roasting vegetables, sautéing proteins, and dressing salads. Its low smoke point also makes it ideal for quick cooking methods that preserve the nutritional value of ingredients.

To get started, try lightly drizzling olive oil over vegetables before roasting or mixing it with lemon juice and herbs for a simple salad dressing. You can also use it as a finishing oil to drizzle over dishes just before serving, which enhances flavor and adds a touch of authenticity to your meals. This versatile oil is both heart-healthy and full of flavor, making it an essential component of Mediterranean-style cooking.

- **Roasting Vegetables for Depth and Sweetness**

Roasting is one of the simplest ways to cook vegetables in Mediterranean cuisine, as it brings out their natural sweetness and creates a pleasing texture. Vegetables like bell peppers, tomatoes, zucchini, and eggplant are ideal for roasting. With a drizzle of olive oil and a sprinkle of herbs, these vegetables can be roasted at high temperatures until they are tender and slightly caramelized.

Roasted vegetables are versatile and can be used in salads, pasta dishes, grain bowls, or served as a side dish. Roasting is also a forgiving method that works well with a variety of seasonings. Simply add salt, pepper, garlic, and herbs like rosemary or thyme to enhance the flavor, and let the oven do the rest. This method is easy to master and adds a richness to vegetables that pairs beautifully with Mediterranean ingredients.

- **Grilling for Authentic Mediterranean Flavor**

Grilling is a central technique in Mediterranean cooking, known for adding a smoky, charred flavor to foods. Whether cooking outdoors or using a grill pan indoors, grilling is a quick and healthy way to prepare proteins like fish, chicken, and lamb, as well as vegetables and even fruits. Traditional Mediterranean foods like kebabs, vegetable skewers, and grilled seafood are simple to prepare and packed with flavor.

To grill Mediterranean-style, marinate proteins and vegetables in olive oil, lemon juice, garlic, and herbs before placing them on the grill. The high heat helps seal in moisture, creating a juicy, tender result. Grilling also adds a depth of flavor that complements the simplicity of Mediterranean ingredients, making it a great technique for anyone looking to replicate the region's vibrant flavors at home.

- **Sautéing with Garlic and Herbs for Quick, Flavorful Dishes**

Sautéing is another essential technique in Mediterranean cooking, used to bring out the flavors of ingredients quickly. Sautéed vegetables, grains, and proteins are commonly found in Mediterranean cuisine, often flavored with garlic, herbs, and a splash of olive oil. This method works well for leafy greens like spinach, as well as for proteins like shrimp or chicken.

To sauté Mediterranean-style, start by heating a small amount of olive oil in a pan. Add garlic and your choice of herbs, and let them cook for a few seconds to release their aromas before adding the main ingredients. This method quickly infuses dishes with flavor and helps retain the texture and nutrients of vegetables. Sautéing is a versatile technique that allows for fast, flavorful meals with minimal cleanup.

- **Marinating for Tenderness and Flavor**

Marinating is a simple yet powerful technique that adds flavor and tenderness to proteins and vegetables. In Mediterranean cuisine, marinades are typically made from olive oil, lemon juice, garlic, and fresh herbs, which penetrate foods with vibrant flavors. Marinating meats, fish, or vegetables for at least 30 minutes can make a big difference in taste and texture, especially when grilling or roasting.

To create a basic Mediterranean marinade, combine olive oil, fresh lemon juice, minced garlic, and herbs like oregano or basil. You can adjust the marinade based on the protein or vegetable you're using. Marinating foods before cooking not only enhances their flavor but also helps preserve their juiciness, resulting in a delicious, Mediterranean-inspired meal.

- **Building Flavor with Fresh Herbs and Citrus**

The Mediterranean diet relies on the natural flavors of fresh herbs and citrus, rather than salt or heavy sauces. Fresh herbs like basil, parsley, mint, and cilantro add brightness and complexity to dishes. Citrus fruits like lemons and oranges are used to enhance the flavor of proteins, grains, and salads, providing a refreshing tang that balances the richness of olive oil.

Using herbs and citrus is simple and requires no cooking skills. Add chopped herbs to dishes just before serving to retain their flavor, or squeeze fresh lemon juice over proteins and vegetables to brighten the dish. These ingredients are easily accessible, making them an effortless way to add Mediterranean flavors to your meals.

- **Adding Depth with Simple Tomato-Based Sauces**

Tomato-based sauces are widely used in Mediterranean cuisine, offering a rich, savory element that complements grains, pasta, and proteins. Simple sauces made from tomatoes, garlic, onions, and herbs are a staple in Mediterranean cooking. These sauces are typically made from scratch, using either fresh or canned tomatoes, and require only a short cooking time to develop a robust flavor.

To make a basic tomato sauce, start by sautéing garlic and onions in olive oil, then add tomatoes and let the mixture simmer until it thickens. Season with herbs like basil or oregano, and finish with a dash of salt and pepper. This sauce can be used as a base for pasta dishes, as a topping for grilled vegetables, or even as a dip for bread. Making homemade tomato sauce is an easy way to add Mediterranean depth to meals without relying on processed ingredients.

- **Embracing Whole Grains and Legumes in One-Pot Meals**

Whole grains and legumes are foundational in Mediterranean cooking, often featured in one-pot meals that combine multiple food groups for a balanced dish. Cooking grains like farro, quinoa, or barley in one pot with vegetables, herbs, and a splash of olive oil creates a hearty, nutritious meal with minimal effort. Legumes, such as lentils or chickpeas, can also be cooked this way, providing plant-based protein and fiber.

One-pot meals are ideal for busy days and can be customized with whatever vegetables or herbs you have on hand. These dishes are easy to prepare and allow the flavors of ingredients to meld together, resulting in a satisfying, Mediterranean-inspired meal. Embracing whole grains and legumes in your cooking routine not only adds nutritional benefits but also introduces diverse flavors and textures to meals.

- **Creating Mediterranean Bowls for Versatile, Balanced Meals**

Mediterranean bowls are a popular way to enjoy a balanced meal that includes grains, vegetables, proteins, and healthy fats. These bowls are highly customizable and can be prepared with minimal cooking. Start by layering a base of whole grains like quinoa or bulgur, add vegetables (either fresh or roasted), top with a protein like grilled chicken or chickpeas, and finish with a drizzle of olive oil and a sprinkle of herbs.

These bowls allow you to mix and match ingredients based on what's in season or readily available, making it easy to incorporate a variety of nutrients into your diet. Mediterranean bowls are not only visually appealing but also convenient for meal prep, offering a nutritious and satisfying option for lunch or dinner.

- **Bringing Mediterranean Cooking Techniques into Your Everyday Life**

Incorporating Mediterranean cooking techniques at home is both achievable and rewarding. By focusing on simple methods like roasting, grilling, marinating, and using fresh herbs, you can enjoy the rich flavors and health benefits of the

Mediterranean diet without complicated recipes or lengthy preparations. These techniques allow the natural flavors of fresh, high-quality ingredients to shine, creating meals that are wholesome, flavorful, and easy to prepare.

With these approachable methods, cooking Mediterranean-style becomes a way to celebrate the goodness of fresh, nourishing foods. By embracing these techniques, you can create meals that not only satisfy your taste buds but also support a balanced, healthy lifestyle inspired by the Mediterranean way of eating.

The importance of fresh, seasonal ingredients

The foundation of the Mediterranean diet rests on the idea of savoring fresh, seasonal ingredients. This emphasis on seasonal produce and unprocessed foods is central to the health benefits and rich flavors associated with Mediterranean cuisine. By focusing on what's fresh and in season, Mediterranean-style eating not only enhances the taste of meals but also supports the body's nutritional needs. Seasonal ingredients are often richer in nutrients and flavor, allowing for a truly satisfying and health-promoting approach to food.

- **Fresh Ingredients and Nutritional Value**

Fresh ingredients are more nutrient-dense than processed or out-of-season options, retaining higher levels of vitamins, minerals, and antioxidants. Foods that are freshly harvested, like ripe tomatoes in the summer or leafy greens in spring, deliver essential nutrients when they're at their peak. Since the Mediterranean diet emphasizes vegetables, fruits, whole grains, and legumes, using fresh ingredients maximizes the nutritional benefits these food groups offer.

Choosing fresh ingredients for every meal helps reduce reliance on preservatives and artificial ingredients, which are often added to extend the shelf life of processed foods. By incorporating fresh vegetables, fruits, and herbs, you can create vibrant meals with the natural flavors of each season. This approach ensures that your body is receiving essential nutrients in their most potent form, contributing to better health and overall vitality.

- **Seasonal Ingredients and Flavor**

Seasonal produce is grown and harvested at its peak, resulting in richer, more robust flavors that enhance every dish. The Mediterranean diet embraces this idea by celebrating fresh, flavorful ingredients without excessive seasoning or artificial additives. A ripe tomato in summer has a sweetness and acidity that out-of-season tomatoes can't match, just as fall vegetables like pumpkin and squash bring an earthy warmth to dishes during colder months.

Cooking with seasonal ingredients allows you to explore a variety of tastes and textures throughout the year, making meals both exciting and satisfying. It encourages you to prepare dishes that highlight the essence of each season, from simple salads in summer to hearty stews in winter. This natural cycle of flavors adds an element of pleasure and variety to your meals, making it easier to enjoy balanced eating year-round.

- **The Health Benefits of Seasonal Eating**

Eating seasonally supports the body's natural nutritional needs, as different fruits and vegetables are available in each season to provide the vitamins and minerals we need most at that time. For instance, in winter, foods high in vitamin C, such as oranges and leafy greens, help boost immunity, while in summer, water-rich foods like cucumbers and melons provide hydration. The Mediterranean diet's focus on seasonal ingredients aligns well with these natural cycles, offering a way to enhance well-being throughout the year.

Additionally, seasonal foods are often more affordable and accessible, as they don't require long-distance transportation or preservation processes. Buying locally grown seasonal produce reduces the environmental impact associated with out-of-season food production, while also providing fresher options that support health. This approach to eating is both eco-friendly and nutritionally aligned with what the body needs as seasons change, making it a holistic choice for long-term wellness.

- **Reducing Food Waste with Fresh, Seasonal Choices**

When we buy seasonal ingredients, we're more likely to consume them quickly, reducing food waste. Fresh ingredients have shorter shelf lives, encouraging us to plan meals around what's available now. In the Mediterranean, it's common to visit local markets several times a week to buy produce for upcoming meals. This practice not only supports local farmers but also helps prevent food waste by buying only what's needed.

Cooking with fresh, seasonal ingredients invites creativity and inspires you to use all parts of a vegetable or fruit in different recipes. For example, root vegetables like carrots can be roasted for a side dish, and their leafy tops can be blended into a pesto. Using ingredients in multiple ways maximizes their value and prevents waste, aligning with Mediterranean principles of sustainability and respect for natural resources.

- **Supporting Local Agriculture and Economy**

The Mediterranean diet is deeply rooted in local agricultural traditions, emphasizing foods that grow naturally in the region. Choosing seasonal ingredients often means selecting local produce, which supports farmers and reduces the carbon footprint associated with transporting food over long distances. By purchasing fresh ingredients from local markets, consumers contribute to their regional economy, creating a mutually beneficial relationship between farmers and the community.

Local produce also tends to be fresher, as it's often harvested at peak ripeness and sold shortly after. This contrasts with imported produce, which may be harvested prematurely to withstand transport. Supporting local agriculture not only promotes fresher, tastier food but also helps maintain biodiversity and preserves the natural landscape, which is integral to the Mediterranean lifestyle and philosophy of eating.

- **Simple Recipes That Highlight Fresh Ingredients**

In Mediterranean cuisine, simplicity is key. Dishes are often prepared to let fresh ingredients shine without masking their natural flavors. Recipes focus on a few high-quality ingredients—like ripe tomatoes, fresh herbs, or a drizzle of olive oil—to create satisfying meals. By letting seasonal produce take center stage, Mediterranean cooking preserves the nutritional integrity and taste of each ingredient, allowing flavors to come alive without overcomplication.

A typical Mediterranean meal might include a fresh salad made with seasonal greens, a main dish of grilled fish or legumes, and a side of roasted vegetables. These meals are simple to prepare yet deeply satisfying, as each ingredient contributes its unique flavor and texture. Cooking with fresh, seasonal produce invites experimentation and allows home cooks to celebrate the natural variety that each season brings.

- **Building a Seasonal Pantry for Mediterranean Cooking**

To fully embrace Mediterranean-style cooking at home, it helps to stock a pantry that complements fresh ingredients. Staples like olive oil, vinegar, herbs, and grains can pair with seasonal produce to create delicious, versatile meals. For instance, grains like farro or couscous can serve as the base for salads or bowls that incorporate whatever fresh ingredients are in season.

Keeping a few essentials on hand allows you to build balanced meals around fresh ingredients, making meal prep faster and more flexible. Having these staples means you can always create a Mediterranean-inspired dish, whether it's a hearty grain salad with seasonal vegetables or a simple pasta tossed with olive oil and fresh tomatoes. With the right pantry basics, cooking with seasonal produce becomes more accessible and enjoyable.

- **Connecting with Nature Through Seasonal Eating**

Eating seasonally allows us to reconnect with nature's rhythms and appreciate the cycle of growth and harvest. The Mediterranean approach to food is centered on celebrating nature's bounty and embracing the beauty of each season. When you choose fresh, seasonal ingredients, you're not only making a nutritional choice but also participating in a tradition that respects the environment and honors the land.

This mindful approach to eating helps cultivate a deeper appreciation for the origins of our food and the work involved in bringing it to the table. It encourages us to slow down, savor each bite, and enjoy meals in harmony with nature. For those seeking a more grounded, meaningful way of eating, seasonal ingredients provide a way to bring mindfulness into everyday meals, just as the Mediterranean lifestyle promotes.

- **Making Fresh, Seasonal Ingredients a Habit**

  Incorporating fresh, seasonal ingredients into your diet doesn't have to be complicated. Visit local farmers' markets, explore what's in season, and plan meals around those ingredients. The Mediterranean approach makes it easy to adjust recipes based on what's available, making each meal an opportunity to enjoy the flavors of the season. Whether it's a summer salad filled with ripe tomatoes and cucumbers or a winter stew with root vegetables, fresh ingredients elevate the dish and provide essential nutrients.

  Embracing fresh, seasonal ingredients brings the Mediterranean philosophy of health, sustainability, and flavor to your kitchen. This practice not only enhances your meals but also fosters a mindful, appreciative relationship with food. By prioritizing what's fresh and in season, you're not just following a diet—you're adopting a way of life that promotes health, environmental responsibility, and culinary enjoyment year-round.

Chapter 5

The Health Benefits of Key Mediterranean Ingredients

Spotlight on ingredients like olive oil, fish, herbs, and nuts and their unique health properties

Olive oil, fish, herbs, and nuts stand out as cornerstones in this diet, offering unique properties that support heart health, reduce inflammation, and contribute to overall wellness. By focusing on these key ingredients, the Mediterranean way of eating fosters a balanced, flavorful approach that prioritizes nutrition, making it both delicious and health-conscious.

* **Olive Oil: The Heart-Healthy Staple**

Olive oil is one of the defining features of Mediterranean cuisine, widely regarded as a "liquid gold" due to its health-boosting properties and versatility in cooking. Rich in monounsaturated fats, particularly oleic acid, olive oil has been shown to improve cholesterol levels and reduce the risk of heart disease. It's also high in antioxidants, such as vitamin E and polyphenols, which help fight inflammation and protect cells from oxidative damage.

Cold-pressed extra virgin olive oil (EVOO) is considered the highest quality due to its minimal processing, which preserves its nutrients and flavor. Using olive oil as a base for salad dressings, marinades, or light sautéing enhances both the taste and nutritional profile of dishes. Studies show that diets high in olive oil are associated with lower risks of stroke, Alzheimer's, and certain cancers, making it an essential ingredient for promoting long-term health.

- **Fish: Lean Protein with Omega-3s**

  Fish, especially fatty fish like salmon, mackerel, and sardines, is a fundamental source of lean protein and omega-3 fatty acids in the Mediterranean diet. Omega-3s are essential fats known for their anti-inflammatory properties, which benefit heart and brain health. These fatty acids help reduce blood pressure, improve blood vessel function, and decrease the risk of blood clots. Regular consumption of omega-3-rich fish has been linked to lower risks of heart disease, stroke, and even depression, as omega-3s play a critical role in brain function and mental well-being.

  The Mediterranean diet typically includes fish at least twice a week, emphasizing the value of seafood over red and processed meats. This approach not only supports cardiovascular health but also offers a clean source of protein that is low in saturated fats. Fish is highly versatile and can be grilled, baked, or added to stews and salads, allowing for flavorful and nourishing meals that provide essential nutrients for overall wellness.

- **Herbs: Nature's Antioxidant Powerhouses**

Herbs like basil, oregano, rosemary, and thyme are much more than just flavor enhancers in Mediterranean cooking—they are rich sources of antioxidants, vitamins, and minerals. These herbs contain polyphenols, compounds that provide strong antioxidant properties, helping to protect the body from free radical damage and inflammation. For instance, rosemary has been studied for its anti-inflammatory effects, while oregano is rich in carvacrol and thymol, natural compounds with antimicrobial and antifungal properties.

Fresh and dried herbs are used abundantly in Mediterranean recipes, adding depth and aroma to dishes while enhancing health. Mint and parsley, frequently found in salads and marinades, provide vitamin K, iron, and fiber. Sage and thyme have long been used in traditional medicine for their potential to improve digestion and support the immune system. Incorporating a variety of herbs into daily meals not only brings out the natural flavors of ingredients but also adds a powerful nutritional boost, making every meal a healing experience.

- **Nuts: Nutrient-Dense Snacks and Meal Enhancers**

Nuts like almonds, walnuts, and pistachios are an important part of the Mediterranean diet, offering plant-based protein, healthy fats, and essential minerals. They are particularly high in monounsaturated and polyunsaturated fats, including omega-3 fatty acids, which help protect the heart by improving cholesterol levels and reducing inflammation. Walnuts, for example, are especially rich in omega-3s, making them a beneficial addition to a diet that aims to support cardiovascular health.

Nuts also contain fiber, which promotes digestive health and helps regulate blood sugar levels, as well as magnesium, which is essential for bone health and energy production. As a snack or as part of salads, yogurt, or grain dishes, nuts provide a satisfying crunch and add nutrient density to meals. Regular nut consumption has been associated with a lower risk of heart disease, type 2 diabetes, and obesity, thanks to their satiating effects and high nutrient content. A handful of nuts can curb hunger between meals and offer a balanced blend of protein, fiber, and healthy fats.

- **The Synergy of These Ingredients in the Mediterranean Diet**

The true power of the Mediterranean diet lies in the combination of these ingredients, which work together to provide a balanced profile of nutrients that support health. Olive oil, fish, herbs, and nuts each play a unique role, but their combined effects offer even greater health benefits. For example, using olive oil to prepare fish or incorporating herbs and nuts into salads creates meals that are both satisfying and nutritionally robust. This synergy of ingredients promotes a holistic approach to eating that fuels the body while protecting against chronic diseases.

Each of these foods has a positive impact on reducing inflammation, managing cholesterol, and providing antioxidants, which contribute to the diet's reputation for longevity and wellness. The Mediterranean diet doesn't focus on restriction or elimination but rather on enjoying nutrient-dense foods that support vitality. By integrating these ingredients into meals, one can enjoy both the culinary and health benefits of the Mediterranean lifestyle.

- **Practical Tips for Including These Ingredients in Daily Meals**

Incorporating olive oil, fish, herbs, and nuts into daily meals can be simple and rewarding. Using olive oil as the primary cooking fat, whether for roasting vegetables, dressing salads, or drizzling over grains, ensures a healthy base for meals. For a nutritious protein source, fish can be baked with herbs or grilled and served with a side of greens and whole grains. Adding fresh herbs to dishes like soups, stews, and salads enhances flavor and offers additional nutrients.

For nuts, a handful can be sprinkled over yogurt, blended into pesto, or enjoyed as a snack. Herbs can be grown fresh at home for easy access and are a cost-effective way to add both flavor and nutrients to every meal. This way of eating allows you to take pleasure in simple, wholesome ingredients that offer diverse culinary possibilities, making it easier to follow a Mediterranean-style diet long-term.

- **Connecting to the Mediterranean Lifestyle Through Ingredient Choices**

Using ingredients like olive oil, fish, herbs, and nuts in everyday meals is a way to embrace the Mediterranean lifestyle, which values balance, health, and enjoyment of food. Each ingredient brings unique qualities that contribute to a balanced diet, reflecting a respect for natural flavors and a commitment to health. By incorporating these foods into daily meals, you can experience the benefits of Mediterranean eating, which is not only delicious but also deeply nourishing for the body and mind.

The Mediterranean approach emphasizes mindful eating and appreciation for the natural goodness of foods. Choosing high-quality olive oil, sourcing fresh fish, and using herbs and nuts thoughtfully elevates both the flavor and nutritional content of meals. This focus on simple, nutrient-rich ingredients is a hallmark of the Mediterranean diet, offering a fulfilling way to eat that celebrates the benefits of whole, natural foods.

Chapter 6

Transitioning to a Mediterranean Diet

Steps to gradually adopt a Mediterranean diet in daily life

Transitioning to a Mediterranean diet can be a fulfilling and health-boosting journey that promotes a balanced approach to food and wellness. This dietary pattern emphasizes fresh, whole foods rich in nutrients, while encouraging mindful and enjoyable eating habits. Here are steps to gradually adopt a Mediterranean diet in your daily life, from small changes in meal composition to the incorporation of traditional Mediterranean ingredients and lifestyle practices.

1. Start with Olive Oil as Your Primary Fat Source

One of the most defining aspects of the Mediterranean diet is the use of olive oil as a primary source of fat. Switching from butter, margarine, or other oils to extra virgin olive oil is a simple yet impactful change. Begin by using olive oil for cooking, roasting vegetables, or as a salad dressing base. Olive oil is packed with healthy monounsaturated fats, which are linked to improved heart health and reduced inflammation. This simple substitution lays a strong foundation for Mediterranean eating, offering both health benefits and flavorful versatility in the kitchen.

2. Increase Your Intake of Fruits and Vegetables

Fruits and vegetables form the core of Mediterranean meals, providing essential vitamins, minerals, and fiber. Aim to fill half of your plate with colorful produce, gradually increasing the variety and quantity of fruits and vegetables in your diet. Incorporate leafy greens, tomatoes, bell peppers, cucumbers, and zucchini into salads, side dishes, and mains. For breakfast, add fruits like berries, oranges, or figs. This steady increase helps build the habit of incorporating nutrient-dense, plant-based foods into each meal, supporting long-term health benefits.

3. Make Whole Grains a Daily Staple

Whole grains like quinoa, farro, bulgur, and brown rice are nutrient-dense alternatives to refined grains, providing complex carbohydrates, fiber, and essential minerals. Start incorporating whole grains by replacing white rice or refined pasta with whole-grain options in your meals. Try oatmeal or whole-grain toast for breakfast and add barley or farro to salads for lunch or dinner. The fiber in whole grains aids in digestion and helps maintain steady energy levels throughout the day, making this transition both healthful and satisfying.

4. Incorporate More Plant-Based Proteins

The Mediterranean diet emphasizes plant-based proteins like legumes, beans, nuts, and seeds. Begin by adding chickpeas, lentils, or black beans to soups, salads, and stews. Try having a meatless meal once or twice a week, relying on plant-based proteins as the main source of protein. Hummus, made from chickpeas, and lentil stews are nutrient-dense options that provide protein and fiber. This gradual shift not only reduces saturated fat intake but also offers the benefits of fiber and a variety of minerals that are key to a balanced diet.

5. Enjoy Fish as Your Main Source of Animal Protein

Seafood is a cornerstone of the Mediterranean diet, especially fatty fish like salmon, sardines, and mackerel, which are rich in heart-healthy omega-3 fatty acids. Aim to incorporate fish into your diet at least twice a week, using it as the primary source of animal protein. Start by replacing one or two weekly meat-based meals with fish, grilling or baking it with olive oil, lemon, and herbs for Mediterranean-inspired flavor. Over time, adding more seafood helps reduce saturated fat intake while introducing beneficial fats that support heart and brain health.

6. Use Herbs and Spices Instead of Salt

To flavor meals, Mediterranean cooking relies heavily on herbs and spices like basil, oregano, rosemary, thyme, and garlic, rather than excessive salt. Gradually experiment with these seasonings to add flavor to your dishes, using fresh or dried herbs in salads, roasted vegetables, and fish marinades. Lemon juice and vinegar also add bright flavors without extra sodium. This approach not only enhances the taste but also boosts the antioxidant content of meals while keeping sodium levels low, which supports heart health.

7. Snack on Nuts, Seeds, and Fresh Produce

Mediterranean snacks are often nutrient-dense and minimally processed. Replace chips, cookies, or other processed snacks with options like almonds, walnuts, and fresh fruits. Nuts and seeds offer healthy fats, protein, and fiber, making them a filling snack option. Keep pre-portioned servings of nuts or fresh fruit like apples, oranges, or grapes on hand for easy snacking. This gradual shift to whole-food snacks provides essential nutrients and keeps you satisfied between meals without relying on empty calories.

8. Make Meals an Enjoyable Social Occasion

In the Mediterranean lifestyle, meals are typically a time for connection and enjoyment, often shared with family and friends. Embrace this approach by setting aside time for sit-down meals, even if it's just one meal a day. Try to slow down, savor each bite, and avoid distractions like phones or screens. Socializing over meals not only enhances enjoyment but also fosters a mindful approach to eating, which can improve digestion and support a positive relationship with food.

9. Drink Water and Enjoy Moderate Red Wine, If Appropriate

Water is the primary beverage in the Mediterranean diet, and red wine is enjoyed in moderation, typically with meals. Replace sugary drinks with water throughout the day to stay hydrated. If you drink alcohol and it fits your health needs, consider a small glass of red wine with dinner, as it contains antioxidants that may benefit heart health when consumed in moderation. However, if you do not drink alcohol, focus on water and herbal teas to stay aligned with the Mediterranean approach.

10. Embrace Mindful, Seasonal Eating

The Mediterranean diet emphasizes eating with the seasons, prioritizing fresh, local ingredients. Start by shopping at farmers' markets or opting for seasonal produce, which is often more flavorful and nutrient-rich. Embrace seasonal cooking by trying new fruits and vegetables as they come into season. This approach helps you connect with the rhythm of nature, encourages variety in your diet, and can make eating more enjoyable and budget-friendly as well.

11. Plan Meals with Balance and Variety in Mind

To sustain a Mediterranean diet, plan balanced meals that incorporate a variety of food groups. Aim for meals that combine vegetables, whole grains, healthy fats, and proteins.

For example, a balanced dinner might include grilled fish, a side of roasted vegetables, a mixed green salad, and a whole-grain side like quinoa or farro. Planning balanced meals in advance makes it easier to maintain the Mediterranean approach in the long term and ensures you're consistently getting a broad range of nutrients.

12. Transition Slowly and Set Realistic Goals

As with any dietary change, the key to successfully adopting a Mediterranean diet is to transition gradually. Set small, manageable goals each week, like adding an extra serving of vegetables or replacing a processed snack with fresh fruit. This progressive approach allows you to form lasting habits without feeling overwhelmed, making it easier to stick to the Mediterranean way of eating over time.

Adopting a Mediterranean diet doesn't happen overnight but is a gradual process of introducing and embracing new habits. By incorporating these steps into your daily life, you can build a balanced and healthful eating pattern that aligns with the Mediterranean approach, promoting both physical and mental well-being through mindful food choices, balanced meals, and enjoyable eating practices.

Tips on swapping out processed foods for fresh, whole foods

1. Replace Packaged Snacks with Fresh Fruit or Nuts

One of the simplest swaps is to replace packaged snacks—like chips, crackers, or granola bars—with fresh fruit, unsalted nuts, or seeds. Fresh fruit provides natural sweetness along with fiber, vitamins, and antioxidants. Nuts and seeds, like almonds or sunflower seeds, offer healthy fats and protein, keeping you satisfied for longer. For added variety, mix fruits and nuts for a convenient, portable snack that's as satisfying as it is nutritious.

2. Opt for Whole Grains Instead of Refined Grains

Processed grains, such as white bread, pasta, and rice, often lack the fiber and nutrients that are retained in whole grains. By choosing whole-grain options like brown rice, quinoa, oats, and whole-wheat pasta, you'll add more fiber and essential minerals to your diet. Whole grains help regulate blood sugar and support digestive health, making them a valuable addition to any meal. Start by gradually substituting half of the refined grains in your meals with whole grains to allow your taste buds time to adjust.

3. Use Fresh Herbs and Spices in Place of Packaged Seasoning Mixes

Many seasoning mixes and marinades are high in sodium and contain additives, preservatives, or artificial flavors. Replace these with fresh herbs and spices like basil, oregano, rosemary, thyme, and garlic to enhance flavors naturally. Experimenting with fresh herbs not only adds vibrant taste but also introduces antioxidants and anti-inflammatory compounds to your meals. Fresh herbs can transform even simple dishes into flavorful, Mediterranean-inspired fare without the need for excess salt or artificial additives.

4. Swap Sugary Beverages for Water or Herbal Tea

Sugary drinks, including sodas and bottled juices, contribute to empty calories without providing significant nutrients. A healthier alternative is water, infused with slices of lemon, cucumber, or fresh mint for natural flavor. Herbal teas, such as chamomile or peppermint, offer a hydrating, caffeine-free option with subtle flavors. Transitioning away from sugary beverages not only supports hydration but also reduces added sugar intake, promoting better energy levels and supporting weight management.

5. Choose Fresh Vegetables Over Canned or Processed Versions

While convenient, canned vegetables often contain added sodium or preservatives. Choose fresh, seasonal vegetables whenever possible, as they retain more of their natural nutrients and flavors. Frozen vegetables can also be a nutritious option since they are often flash-frozen at peak ripeness. Fresh vegetables can be prepared in various ways— grilled, roasted, steamed, or eaten raw—allowing you to enjoy their natural flavors while benefiting from vitamins, fiber, and antioxidants.

6. Replace Processed Meats with Lean, Fresh Proteins

Processed meats, like deli slices, sausages, and bacon, are often high in sodium, saturated fat, and preservatives. A healthier choice is to focus on fresh, lean proteins like chicken, turkey, eggs, or seafood, particularly fatty fish like salmon or sardines, which are rich in heart-healthy omega-3 fatty acids. Not only do these fresh protein sources reduce intake of harmful additives, but they also provide essential nutrients that support muscle health, brain function, and overall wellness.

7. Try Homemade Dressings Instead of Store-Bought Versions

Store-bought dressings and sauces often contain added sugars, unhealthy oils, and preservatives. Making your own dressing with ingredients like olive oil, balsamic vinegar, mustard, lemon juice, and herbs is a quick and easy way to keep salads healthy and flavorful. A simple homemade vinaigrette can be whisked together in minutes and tailored to your taste. This swap allows you to control the quality of ingredients and experiment with flavors that suit Mediterranean-inspired dishes.

8. Cook with Fresh Ingredients Instead of Relying on Packaged Meals

Packaged meals are convenient but often contain high levels of sodium, sugars, and unhealthy fats. Preparing meals from scratch allows you to use whole, fresh ingredients and avoid artificial additives. Plan simple, balanced meals with a few key ingredients—like roasted vegetables, grilled fish or chicken, and a side of whole grains. Preparing food at home can become a rewarding routine that allows you to fully enjoy the fresh, vibrant flavors of Mediterranean cooking.

9. Use Natural Sweeteners in Place of Refined Sugars

Instead of using refined sugars, experiment with natural sweeteners like honey, maple syrup, or fruit puree in recipes and beverages. For example, adding a touch of honey to oatmeal or stirring a few slices of apple or berries into yogurt can satisfy a sweet craving without processed sugar. This approach reduces added sugars, helps stabilize blood sugar levels, and keeps treats flavorful and enjoyable without excessive sweetness.

10. Focus on Whole Foods for Each Meal Component

Build your meals around whole food components: choose a fresh protein source, a whole grain, and plenty of vegetables or legumes. For example, instead of a frozen pizza, make a bowl with quinoa, roasted vegetables, leafy greens, chickpeas, and a sprinkle of feta cheese. This balanced approach simplifies the process of meal planning and encourages a variety of flavors and textures that align with the Mediterranean way of eating.

Swapping processed foods for fresh, whole foods can transform both the nutritional profile and the flavor of your meals. As you gradually incorporate these tips, you'll notice not only an improvement in taste but also enhanced energy, better digestion, and a more positive relationship with food. Adopting a Mediterranean approach with whole foods brings enjoyment and mindfulness to eating, allowing you to savor the true essence of each ingredient and its unique health benefits.

Chapter 7

Recipes

Greek Yogurt Parfait

About the recipe: A simple, protein-packed breakfast featuring Greek yogurt, fresh fruit, and a drizzle of honey for a classic Mediterranean start to the day.

Number of servings: 2

Preparation time: 5 minutes

Cooking time: None

Ingredients:

- 1 cup Greek yogurt

- 1/2 cup fresh berries (strawberries, blueberries, or raspberries)

- 1/4 cup granola

- 1 tbsp honey

- 1 tbsp chopped walnuts (optional)

Directions:

1. Divide the Greek yogurt between two serving bowls.

2. Layer fresh berries on top of the yogurt.

3. Sprinkle granola evenly over each bowl.

4. Drizzle honey and add walnuts for extra crunch, if desired.

Nutritional value:

- Calories: 280

- Protein: 14g

- Carbohydrates: 35g

- Fat: 10g

Mediterranean Breakfast Bowl

About the recipe: A savory breakfast bowl filled with wholesome Mediterranean ingredients like eggs, tomatoes, cucumbers, and olives.

Number of servings: 2

Preparation time: 10 minutes

Cooking time: 10 minutes

Ingredients:

- 2 eggs
- 1/2 cup cherry tomatoes, halved
- 1/2 cup cucumber, diced
- 1/4 cup Kalamata olives, sliced

- 1/4 cup feta cheese, crumbled

- 1 tbsp olive oil

- Salt and pepper to taste

- Fresh herbs (parsley or mint), chopped

Directions:

1. Boil or poach the eggs as desired.

2. Divide tomatoes, cucumbers, olives, and feta between two bowls.

3. Drizzle olive oil over the vegetables, and season with salt and pepper.

4. Top each bowl with an egg and sprinkle fresh herbs.

Nutritional value:

- Calories: 300

- Protein: 12g

- Carbohydrates: 14g

- Fat: 23g

Spinach and Feta Frittata

About the recipe: This baked frittata features the Mediterranean flavors of spinach, feta, and herbs.

Number of servings: 4

Preparation time: 10 minutes

Cooking time: 25 minutes

Ingredients:

- 6 large eggs

- 1/2 cup crumbled feta cheese

- 1 cup fresh spinach, chopped

- 1/4 cup milk

- Salt and pepper to taste

- 1 tbsp olive oil

- Fresh herbs (parsley or dill), chopped

Directions:

1. Preheat oven to 350°F (175°C).

2. In a mixing bowl, whisk together eggs, milk, salt, and pepper.

3. Heat olive oil in a skillet over medium heat, and add spinach. Cook until wilted.

4. Pour egg mixture over spinach and sprinkle feta on top.

5. Bake for 20-25 minutes, until the frittata is set.

6. Garnish with fresh herbs and serve.

Nutritional value:

- Calories: 200

- Protein: 14g

- Carbohydrates: 5g

- Fat: 14g

Chickpea Salad with Cucumber and Tomato

About the recipe: A light, refreshing salad filled with the flavors of fresh vegetables, chickpeas, and a lemon-olive oil dressing.

Number of servings: 4

Preparation time: 15 minutes

Cooking time: None

Ingredients:

- 1 can chickpeas, drained and rinsed

- 1 cup cherry tomatoes, halved

- 1 cucumber, diced

- 1/4 red onion, diced

- 1/4 cup Kalamata olives, sliced

- 1/4 cup fresh parsley, chopped

- 3 tbsp olive oil

- Juice of 1 lemon

- Salt and pepper to taste

Directions:

1. In a large mixing bowl, combine chickpeas, tomatoes, cucumber, red onion, olives, and parsley.

2. In a small bowl, whisk together olive oil, lemon juice, salt, and pepper.

3. Pour dressing over the salad and toss to coat.

4. Serve immediately or chill in the fridge for 15 minutes.

Nutritional value:

- Calories: 220

- Protein: 6g

- Carbohydrates: 20g

- Fat: 12g

Mediterranean Quinoa Salad

About the recipe: A hearty quinoa salad mixed with olives, tomatoes, cucumber, and feta, ideal for a nutritious lunch.

Number of servings: 4

Preparation time: 15 minutes

Cooking time: 15 minutes

Ingredients:

- 1 cup quinoa

- 2 cups water

- 1/2 cup cherry tomatoes, halved

- 1/2 cucumber, diced

- 1/4 cup Kalamata olives, sliced

- 1/4 cup crumbled feta cheese

- 3 tbsp olive oil

- Juice of 1 lemon

- Salt and pepper to taste

- Fresh parsley, chopped

Directions:

1. Rinse quinoa and cook in water according to package instructions.

2. Allow quinoa to cool, then transfer to a mixing bowl.

3. Add tomatoes, cucumber, olives, and feta to the quinoa.

4. In a small bowl, whisk olive oil, lemon juice, salt, and pepper, then pour over the salad.

5. Garnish with fresh parsley and serve.

Nutritional value:

*   Calories: 250

*   Protein: 8g

*   Carbohydrates: 30g

*   Fat: 10g

Hummus Wrap

About the recipe: A quick and satisfying hummus wrap with fresh vegetables, perfect for a light Mediterranean-style lunch.

Number of servings: 2

Preparation time: 10 minutes

Cooking time: None

Ingredients:

- 2 large whole-grain wraps

- 1/2 cup hummus

- 1/2 cucumber, thinly sliced

- 1/2 cup spinach leaves

- 1/4 cup cherry tomatoes, halved

- 1/4 cup grated carrots

- Salt and pepper to taste

Directions:

1. Spread hummus evenly over each wrap.

2. Layer cucumber, spinach, cherry tomatoes, and carrots on top of the hummus.

3. Season with salt and pepper if desired.

4. Roll up each wrap tightly and slice in half.

Nutritional value:

- Calories: 280

- Protein: 8g

- Carbohydrates: 35g

- Fat: 12g

Greek Moussaka

About the recipe: A hearty, traditional Greek dish with layers of eggplant, ground meat, and béchamel sauce.

Number of servings: 6

Preparation time: 30 minutes

Cooking time: 1 hour

Ingredients:

- 2 large eggplants, sliced

- 1 lb ground beef or lamb

- 1 onion, diced

- 1 can crushed tomatoes

- 1/2 cup grated cheese

- 1/4 cup olive oil

- Salt and pepper to taste

- Béchamel sauce (made with 2 cups milk, 2 tbsp butter, 2 tbsp flour)

Directions:

1. Preheat oven to 375°F (190°C).

2. Lightly fry eggplant slices in olive oil until tender, and set aside.

3. Brown ground meat with onion, add crushed tomatoes, salt, and pepper.

4. Prepare béchamel sauce: melt butter, whisk in flour, and slowly add milk until thickened.

5. Layer eggplant, meat, and béchamel in a baking dish, and top with grated cheese.

6. Bake for 40 minutes, until golden and bubbly.

Nutritional value:

- Calories: 350

- Protein: 20g

- Carbohydrates: 20g

- Fat: 20g

Shakshuka

About the recipe: Shakshuka is a flavorful Middle Eastern breakfast dish with poached eggs in a spiced tomato and pepper sauce.

Number of servings: 4

Preparation time: 10 minutes

Cooking time: 20 minutes

Ingredients:

- 1 tbsp olive oil

- 1 onion, diced

- 1 red bell pepper, diced

- 3 garlic cloves, minced

- 1 can diced tomatoes

- 1 tsp ground cumin

- 1/2 tsp paprika

- Salt and pepper to taste

- 4 eggs

- Fresh parsley, chopped

Directions:

1. Heat olive oil in a skillet, add onion, and cook until softened.

2. Add bell pepper, garlic, and spices, cooking until fragrant.

3. Pour in the diced tomatoes, season with salt and pepper, and simmer for 10 minutes.

4. Make four small wells in the sauce and crack an egg into each.

5. Cover and cook until eggs are set to your preference, then garnish with parsley.

Nutritional value:

- Calories: 150

- Protein: 8g

- Carbohydrates: 10g

- Fat: 10g

Mediterranean Avocado Toast

About the recipe: A twist on avocado toast with Mediterranean flavors, including tomatoes, feta, and olives.

Number of servings: 2

Preparation time: 5 minutes

Cooking time: None

Ingredients:

- 2 slices whole-grain bread

- 1 avocado, mashed

- 1/4 cup cherry tomatoes, diced

- 2 tbsp crumbled feta cheese

- 1 tbsp Kalamata olives, chopped

- Salt and pepper to taste

- Fresh basil or parsley, chopped

Directions:

1. Toast bread slices to desired crispiness.

2. Spread mashed avocado evenly over each slice.

3. Top with tomatoes, feta, and olives, then season with salt and pepper.

4. Garnish with fresh herbs and serve immediately.

Nutritional value:

- Calories: 250

- Protein: 6g

- Carbohydrates: 24g

- Fat: 15g

Greek Lentil Soup (Fakes)

About the recipe: A nutritious and filling Greek lentil soup with flavors of garlic, bay leaves, and a dash of red wine vinegar for a hearty lunch.

Number of servings: 4

Preparation time: 10 minutes

Cooking time: 30 minutes

Ingredients:

- 1 cup brown lentils
- 4 cups water
- 1 onion, chopped

- 2 garlic cloves, minced

- 2 bay leaves

- 1 can diced tomatoes

- 2 tbsp olive oil

- Salt and pepper to taste

- 1 tbsp red wine vinegar

Directions:

1. In a pot, heat olive oil, add onion and garlic, and cook until softened.

2. Add lentils, bay leaves, diced tomatoes, and water.

3. Simmer for 25-30 minutes until lentils are tender.

4. Season with salt, pepper, and red wine vinegar just before serving.

Nutritional value:

- Calories: 180

- Protein: 12g

- Carbohydrates: 28g

- Fat: 5g

Mediterranean Stuffed Bell Peppers

About the recipe: Colorful bell peppers stuffed with quinoa, vegetables, and feta for a balanced Mediterranean lunch.

Number of servings: 4

Preparation time: 15 minutes

Cooking time: 30 minutes

Ingredients:

- 4 large bell peppers

- 1 cup cooked quinoa

- 1/2 cup cherry tomatoes, diced

- 1/4 cup Kalamata olives, chopped

- 1/4 cup feta cheese, crumbled

- 2 tbsp fresh parsley, chopped

- Salt and pepper to taste

Directions:

1. Preheat oven to 375°F (190°C).

2. Cut the tops off peppers and remove seeds.

3. In a bowl, mix cooked quinoa, tomatoes, olives, feta, parsley, salt, and pepper.

4. Stuff each pepper with the mixture and place in a baking dish.

5. Cover with foil and bake for 30 minutes until peppers are tender.

Nutritional value:

- Calories: 200

- Protein: 6g

- Carbohydrates: 25g

- Fat: 8g

Grilled Chicken Souvlaki

About the recipe: Chicken souvlaki marinated in Greek spices and served with a side of tzatziki for a delicious, flavorful dinner.

Number of servings: 4

Preparation time: 15 minutes (plus marinating time)

Cooking time: 15 minutes

Ingredients:

- 1 lb chicken breast, cut into cubes

- 2 tbsp olive oil

- Juice of 1 lemon

- 2 garlic cloves, minced

- 1 tsp dried oregano

- Salt and pepper to taste

Directions:

1. In a bowl, mix olive oil, lemon juice, garlic, oregano, salt, and pepper.

2. Add chicken cubes to marinade, cover, and refrigerate for at least 1 hour.

3. Thread chicken onto skewers and grill over medium heat for 10-15 minutes until cooked through.

Nutritional value:

- Calories: 180

- Protein: 25g

- Carbohydrates: 2g

- Fat: 8g

Seafood Paella

About the recipe: A Mediterranean take on paella with fresh shrimp, mussels, and vegetables for a flavorful, family-style dinner.

Number of servings: 6

Preparation time: 20 minutes

Cooking time: 40 minutes

Ingredients:

- 1 tbsp olive oil

- 1 onion, diced

- 2 garlic cloves, minced

- 1 bell pepper, diced

- 1 cup Arborio rice

- 1/4 cup white wine

- 3 cups chicken or seafood broth

- 1/2 lb shrimp, peeled and deveined

- 1/2 lb mussels, cleaned

- 1/2 cup green peas

- Salt and pepper to taste

- Fresh parsley, chopped

Directions:

1. Heat olive oil in a large skillet, add onion, garlic, and bell pepper, and sauté until softened.

2. Add rice and cook for 1 minute.

3. Pour in white wine and let it absorb, then add broth.

4. Simmer for 15 minutes, then add shrimp, mussels, and peas, and cook until seafood is done.

5. Season with salt, pepper, and parsley before serving.

Nutritional value:

- Calories: 300

- Protein: 20g

- Carbohydrates: 35g

- Fat: 8g

Eggplant and Chickpea Stew

About the recipe: A hearty vegetarian stew with eggplant, chickpeas, and Mediterranean spices for a comforting dinner.

Number of servings: 4

Preparation time: 15 minutes

Cooking time: 40 minutes

Ingredients:

- 1 tbsp olive oil

- 1 large eggplant, diced

- 1 onion, diced

- 2 garlic cloves, minced

- 1 can chickpeas, drained and rinsed

- 1 can diced tomatoes

- 1 tsp ground cumin

- Salt and pepper to taste

- Fresh parsley, chopped

Directions:

1. Heat olive oil in a pot, add eggplant and onion, and cook until softened.

2. Add garlic, chickpeas, tomatoes, and cumin, and season with salt and pepper.

3. Simmer for 30 minutes, stirring occasionally.

4. Garnish with fresh parsley and serve.

Nutritional value:

- Calories: 200

- Protein: 6g

- Carbohydrates: 30g

- Fat: 8g

Falafel Salad Bowl

About the recipe: A fresh, vibrant salad bowl featuring homemade falafel, crisp vegetables, and a creamy tahini dressing for a delicious and nutritious lunch.

Number of servings: 4

Preparation time: 20 minutes (plus soaking time for chickpeas)

Cooking time: 15 minutes

Ingredients:

For the falafel:

- 1 cup dried chickpeas, soaked overnight

- 1/2 onion, roughly chopped

- 2 cloves garlic, minced

- 1/4 cup fresh parsley, chopped

- 1 tsp ground cumin

- 1 tsp ground coriander

- Salt and pepper to taste

- 2 tbsp olive oil for frying

For the salad:

- 4 cups mixed greens

- 1 cucumber, sliced

- 1 cup cherry tomatoes, halved

- 1/4 cup Kalamata olives

- 1/4 cup crumbled feta cheese (optional)

For the dressing:

- 2 tbsp tahini

- Juice of 1 lemon

- 1 tbsp water (to thin, if necessary)

- Salt and pepper to taste

Directions:

1. To make falafel, combine chickpeas, onion, garlic, parsley, cumin, coriander, salt, and pepper in a food processor. Pulse until well combined but not pureed.

2. Shape mixture into small balls and flatten slightly.

3. Heat olive oil in a pan over medium heat, and fry falafel until golden brown on each side.

4. Arrange mixed greens, cucumber, cherry tomatoes, olives, and feta in bowls.

5. Add falafel on top and drizzle with tahini dressing made by whisking tahini, lemon juice, water, salt, and pepper.

Nutritional value:

- Calories: 350

- Protein: 12g

- Carbohydrates: 40g

- Fat: 15g

Lemon Herb Grilled Salmon

About the recipe: A simple and delicious Mediterranean-inspired grilled salmon dish with a lemon-herb marinade, perfect for a light dinner.

Number of servings: 4

Preparation time: 10 minutes (plus marinating time)

Cooking time: 10 minutes

Ingredients:

- 4 salmon fillets

- 3 tbsp olive oil

- Juice and zest of 1 lemon

- 2 garlic cloves, minced

- 1 tbsp fresh dill, chopped

- 1 tbsp fresh parsley, chopped

- Salt and pepper to taste

Directions:

1. In a bowl, mix olive oil, lemon juice and zest, garlic, dill, parsley, salt, and pepper.

2. Place salmon fillets in a dish, pour marinade over, and let sit for 15-20 minutes.

3. Preheat grill to medium-high heat. Grill salmon fillets for 4-5 minutes per side, until cooked through.

4. Serve with a side of vegetables or a simple salad.

Nutritional value:

- Calories: 300

- Protein: 25g

- Carbohydrates: 2g

- Fat: 20g

Olive and Feta Breakfast Muffins

About the recipe: These savory muffins are perfect for a quick, on-the-go Mediterranean breakfast. Filled with olives, feta, and fresh herbs, they're packed with flavor.

Number of servings: 6 muffins

Preparation time: 10 minutes

Cooking time: 20 minutes

Ingredients:

- 1 cup all-purpose flour

- 1/2 tsp baking powder

- 1/4 tsp salt

- 2 large eggs

- 1/2 cup Greek yogurt

- 1/4 cup olive oil

- 1/2 cup crumbled feta cheese

- 1/4 cup Kalamata olives, chopped

- 2 tbsp fresh parsley, chopped

Directions:

1. Preheat oven to 350°F (175°C) and grease a muffin tin.

2. In a bowl, mix flour, baking powder, and salt.

3. In a separate bowl, whisk together eggs, Greek yogurt, and olive oil until smooth.

4. Fold in feta, olives, and parsley, then add the dry ingredients and mix until just combined.

5. Pour batter into muffin tin, filling each cup about 3/4 full.

6. Bake for 20 minutes or until a toothpick comes out clean.

Nutritional value:

- Calories: 180

- Protein: 5g

- Carbohydrates: 10g

- Fat: 12g

Greek Orzo Salad with Shrimp

About the recipe: This light and refreshing Greek orzo salad is perfect for lunch, featuring juicy shrimp, fresh vegetables, and a tangy lemon dressing.

Number of servings: 4

Preparation time: 10 minutes

Cooking time: 10 minutes

Ingredients:

- 1 cup orzo pasta

- 1/2 lb shrimp, peeled and deveined

- 1 tbsp olive oil

- Salt and pepper to taste

- 1/2 cup cherry tomatoes, halved

- 1/2 cucumber, diced

- 1/4 cup Kalamata olives, sliced

- 1/4 cup crumbled feta cheese

- Fresh parsley, chopped

For the dressing:

- 2 tbsp olive oil

- Juice of 1 lemon

- 1 garlic clove, minced

- Salt and pepper to taste

Directions:

1. Cook orzo according to package instructions, drain, and let cool.

2. In a skillet, heat olive oil and cook shrimp until pink, seasoning with salt and pepper.

3. In a large bowl, combine orzo, shrimp, tomatoes, cucumber, olives, feta, and parsley.

4. In a small bowl, whisk together olive oil, lemon juice, garlic, salt, and pepper, then pour over the salad and toss.

Nutritional value:

- Calories: 320

- Protein: 20g

- Carbohydrates: 32g

- Fat: 12g

Stuffed Eggplant with Ground Beef and Pine Nuts

About the recipe: This Mediterranean-inspired stuffed eggplant is rich, flavorful, and perfect for dinner. Ground beef, pine nuts, and spices bring out warm, aromatic flavors.

Number of servings: 4

Preparation time: 15 minutes

Cooking time: 30 minutes

Ingredients:

- 2 medium eggplants, halved lengthwise

- 2 tbsp olive oil

- 1/2 lb ground beef

- 1 onion, diced

- 2 garlic cloves, minced

- 1/4 cup pine nuts

- 1/2 tsp ground cinnamon

- Salt and pepper to taste

- Fresh parsley, chopped

Directions:

1. Preheat oven to 375°F (190°C). Scoop out the centers of each eggplant half, creating a "boat," and brush with olive oil. Bake for 10-15 minutes until slightly tender.

2. Meanwhile, in a skillet, cook ground beef, onion, garlic, pine nuts, cinnamon, salt, and pepper until beef is browned and onions are soft.

3. Fill each eggplant half with the beef mixture and return to the oven for 15 minutes.

4. Garnish with parsley and serve hot.

Nutritional value:

- Calories: 320

- Protein: 15g

- Carbohydrates: 10g

- Fat: 25g

Conclusion

As we reach the end of our journey through the Mediterranean way of life, it's clear that this isn't just a diet—it's a philosophy, a celebration, and a lifestyle rooted in balance, connection, and joy. The Mediterranean diet invites us to slow down, savor, and embrace the simple pleasures of fresh, nourishing food shared in good company. It offers us a path to health not through restriction or rigidity, but through abundant flavors, textures, and the profound satisfaction that comes from eating well.

Throughout this book, we've explored the history, science, and heart of the Mediterranean diet. From its roots in ancient civilizations to the latest scientific findings, we've seen how this way of eating supports both physical and mental health. It's a lifestyle that doesn't just sustain us—it enriches us. The benefits reach beyond the physical, touching our minds and spirits as we learn to appreciate food as a source of pleasure, vitality, and well-being.

As you set out to incorporate Mediterranean habits into your life, remember that this is a personal journey. There's no need to adopt every aspect of the diet overnight. Instead, start with small changes: perhaps begin by incorporating more fresh vegetables, choosing whole grains, or switching to olive oil. Experiment with new recipes, explore local farmers' markets, or invite friends over for a leisurely, homemade meal. Let each step be one of discovery, guided by curiosity and enjoyment.

The beauty of the Mediterranean diet is its flexibility and its adaptability to individual needs and tastes. Whether you're cooking for one or feeding a family, eating on a budget or exploring new ingredients, the principles of Mediterranean eating can support you. With time, these small steps will form lasting habits, turning meals into moments of nourishment and joy.

Above all, let this way of eating remind you of the profound connection between food and life. In every meal, there is an opportunity to nourish not just the body but the soul, to cultivate happiness, and to deepen your connection to the world around you. This, perhaps, is the greatest gift the Mediterranean lifestyle offers: a reminder that health is not only about what we eat but about how we live, love, and connect.

So, here's to a lifetime of joyful, healthful eating. Here's to making each meal an expression of gratitude for the food, the land, and the people who make it all possible. In the end, the

Mediterranean diet is not just a recipe for health—it's a recipe for a life well-lived. May your journey be delicious, nourishing, and filled with joy.

Made in United States
Troutdale, OR
04/11/2025

30522757R00120